Other titles in the *Commercial Contracts for Managers Series*:

Commercial Contracts for Managers Series

UNDERSTANDING EFFECTIVE CONTRACT EVALUATION

by

Frank Adoranti

Dip Law (BAB), MBA (UNE), FCIS

Solicitor and Barrister of the Supreme Court of
New South Wales

Chartered Secretary

Notary Public

GLOBAL
professional
publishing

First published in Great Britain. 2009

Apart from any fair dealing for the purpose of research or private study, or criticism or review, as permitted under the Copyright, Designs and Patents Act 1988, this publication may only be reproduced, stored or transmitted, in any form or by any means, with the prior permission in writing of the publisher, or in the case of reprographic reproduction in accordance with the terms and licences issued by the Copyright Licensing Agency. Enquiries concerning reproduction outside those terms should be addressed to the publisher. The address is below:

GLOBAL PROFESSIONAL PUBLISHING Limited
Random Acres
Slip Mill Lane
Hawkhurst
Cranborne
Kent TN18 5AD

GLOBAL PROFESSIONAL PUBLISHING believes that the sources of information upon which the book is based are reliable, and has made every effort to ensure the complete accuracy of the text. However, neither GLOBAL PROFESSIONAL PUBLISHING , the author nor any contributor can accept any legal responsibility whatsoever for consequences that may arise from errors or omissions or any opinion or advice given.

© Frank Adoranti, 2009

ISBN: 978-0-85297-773-6

Senior editor: Jessica Perini

Cover Designer: Insignia Graphics

Printed by Good News Press

PREFACE

Just because you've been signing contracts for years, it doesn't mean you have understood what you've been signing.

One of management's biggest fears is that of an employee exposing the company to the risk of potentially ruinous litigation. It is a fear with genuine foundation.

The cost of litigation is measured in the billions (indeed one estimate is that in the USA alone, the cost is in excess of US$200 billion).

A company exposed to litigation suffers the following consequences:

1. uncertainty;

2. adverse publicity and loss of reputation; and

3. expense and drain of management time.

These consequences are the natural enemies of the manager. They undermine the marketplace's perception of the company and can also have adverse effects on a company's share price. This is going to be especially so in the post-2008 global-financial-crisis era of business, where a publicly listed corporation can ill-afford to suffer any large-scale loss of confidence by the market.

During the last decade, I have devoted much time and effort to instilling a culture of litigation prevention in corporations, by the education of managers in fundamental concepts of commercial contracts.

A common question raised by managers at the conclusion of my seminars or presentations is: *What book can I read as a ready reference?* Unfortunately, I found no particular book catering to these aspects of corporate legal education. The most common problems expressed to me regarding existing books on the market were that they were:

- **too difficult to read:** the bulk of titles on the market dealing with contracts are scholarly academic works intended for the practising lawyer or law student;

- **not practical:** the less imposing and shorter "guides" are predominantly aimed at law students "cramming" or revising for examinations or oriented to consumer law issues (neighbourhood disputes, family law, wills and personal bankruptcy); and

- **not portable:** none are presented as handy reference guides specifically tailored to managers. They are usually off-putting in their size, length and/ or prohibitive expense.

When discussing the concept of a managers' guide to commercial contracts, most of the comments I received from managers can be summarised in the following quotation:

Whilst it might not offer the depth of information on a particular topic that a textbook does, a handy guide in your briefcase accessible <u>when you need it</u> is far better than the volumes sitting on a shelf back at your home or office.

This provided me with the final impetus to fill the need in this area. You hold in your hands the sixth and final volume in a series of books catering to this requirement.

Many organisations are constantly on the search for new business – therefore tendering or contract reviews and evaluations are, for many of them, an everyday occurrence.

To the non-lawyer, commercial contracts (like many legal documents) are often shrouded in mystery. The documents are becoming increasingly unwieldy as they attempt to weave complex structures of rules and protocols. This is especially so as contracts tend to outsource more risk to contractors and cater for a large number of contingencies.

The purpose of this book is to provide an explanation of their function and operation as well as clear demonstrations illustrating the effects of the attempts to outsource sometimes disproportionate amount of risk to contractors. The aim is to help companies understand such issues and ultimately avoid the aggravation of contract disputes and litigation.

Along the way, you will find a number of practical tips on some of the traps and pitfalls of contract evaluation.

As a safeguard, you should *always* seek qualified legal advice in specific situations.

When dealing with the law, often, there is no single "right" answer. This series of books will help managers develop the ability to deal with particular aspects of the ambiguities of contracts. They should be of assistance to every manager dealing with commercial contracts and agreements and from sales and business development staff through to the CEO and CFO. The series caters to those in large publicly-listed organisations as well as to smaller businesses.

In writing this series, I have drawn on over 20 years of experience in the law in various countries. I have tried to cut through the mire of theory and "legalese" and distil the essence of a highly technical topic into something easily understandable and digestible for the manager in a hurry.

Where possible, I have used actual examples, based on situations I have advised upon, as illustrations of many of the points made in the book. Obviously, the names and situations have been altered to make the actual participants unidentifiable.

I trust you find this series of guides as useful to read as I found them enjoyable to write.

Frank Adoranti
Sydney, December 2008

ACKNOWLEDGMENTS

Naturally, a work which is the product of many years of research and development never comes together single-handedly.

I wish to thank Peta De Michele and Sandra Brzoska for their reviews and helpful comments on the manuscript. Thanks Sandra for the constant and helpful "reminders" to prioritise the completion of this work – otherwise, it could well have ended up becoming a 22nd century publication!

To my editor, Jessica Perini, wow! Who would have ever thought we'd get this far – the entire six books of the series. You are the consummate professional. Always there to offer the appropriate guidance and encouragement needed to achieve the task.

To my brother Gino for his friendship and support.

To my parents, for their total love – they will always be my treasures.

Finally, to my wife Rosalie, always the centre of my universe and brilliant mother to our incredibly delightful (and increasingly mischievous) children: Kiara, Gianni, Luca and Serena.

ABOUT THE AUTHOR

The author commenced working in the private practice of law over 20 years ago. Since 1996 he has worked with a number of multinational corporations both in Europe and in the Asia–Pacific region.

As an international corporate lawyer and consultant, he has reviewed thousands of significant commercial agreements and has seen, first hand, the damage that organisations suffer when proper care is not exercised in negotiating and correctly documenting contract terms. He has also conducted and managed hundreds of millions of dollars of litigation in various parts of the world, caused by such lack of care.

For many years, contract evaluations have been a daily (and very often, nightly) part of his life.

He has been involved in a broad range of commercial transactions ranging from the acquisition and sale of international companies to simple confidentiality agreements, and much else in between. He has also assisted organisations with:

- mergers and acquisitions;

- post-merger integrations;
- corporate restructures;
- establishment of tender and bidding processes;
- crisis management planning;
- contract management systems;
- legal audit and legal risk assessments;
- relations with external lawyers;
- planning corporate legal departments;
- compliance programs; and
- in-house training programs and seminars on contracts and other legal issues.

In addition to his qualifications as a lawyer, he has an MBA and is a Fellow of the Institute of Chartered Secretaries and Administrators. He is also a Notary Public.

TABLE OF CONTENTS

Part 1

THE MICRO PERSPECTIVE

INTRODUCTION

This book will give managers and employees an understanding of how organisations can review and evaluate contracts in the course of business.

For many organisations, effective contract evaluation goes to the very foundations of their operations and revenue streams. For this reason, it is important that organisations involved in either or both these processes have an understanding of the various options of contract evaluation methods available to them. They will also need to be armed with information on the way to select the most appropriate method best suited to their philosophies and needs.

Parties will attempt to transfer as much risk to you as you will allow them to do. Accepting risk has a value – if you take on more than your fair share, you must ensure you are being adequately rewarded.

As more risk is being transferred in contracts, organisations need to delve further into their tool bags to search for ways of better handling and mitigating those risks. The following diagram provides a basic illustration of the point:

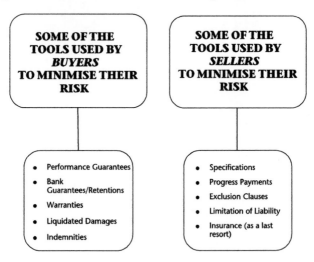

SOME OF THE TOOLS USED BY *BUYERS* TO MINIMISE THEIR RISK	**SOME OF THE TOOLS USED BY *SELLERS* TO MINIMISE THEIR RISK**
• Performance Guarantees • Bank Guarantees/Retentions • Warranties • Liquidated Damages • Indemnities	• Specifications • Progress Payments • Exclusion Clauses • Limitation of Liability • Insurance (as a last resort)

As contract documents become larger and more complex, the time that organisations have to review them is becoming shorter. Under such constraints and with the constant pressure to win business, managers are tempted to take fewer precautions and more unnecessary risks.

Directors must ensure that adequate processes and systems are in place to ensure that a balance is achieved between winning new business and capitalising on new opportunities and not inadvertently committing an organisation to unduly onerous provisions or accepting an inordinately high level of risk.

Such processes will also help prevent an organisation from inadvertently "wandering off course".

Golden Nugget

In contract evaluation, *preventative* measures and safeguards are the best tools available.

- Often, an organisation's liability problem can be traced back to the actual *negotiation* of the contract.

- The efforts companies devote to addressing liability issues can be categorised as follows:

  - **BEFORE** CONTRACT EXECUTION
    » It's called *Risk Management*
  - **AFTER** CONTRACT EXECUTION
    » It sometimes becomes *Crisis Management*

You will also learn a number of different ways that an organisation can create or streamline both processes so that they become systematised. As the book unfolds, the reader will begin to understand how both processes are intricately connected and how the proper management of *both* is essential.

Organisations deal with contract issues almost every day. They can be in the form of tenders, distribution agreements, sub-contracts or even confidentiality agreements, or a lease on a piece of office equipment. Such contracts (and many others) form a part of everyday business life.

However, not all managers and employees understand the nuances of contract documents.

Indeed, many have been encountering them for years, sometimes without an appreciation of their full significance and potential ramifications – for example, when one blindly accepts the trading terms of a customer, as contained in their purchase order form.

Golden Nugget

A Broader Approach

When reviewing contracts, look beyond the printed words on the contract document itself, to consider:

- Possible disputes that may arise

- Where those disputes may arise (which country?)

- Avenues of recourse available if the other side refuses to honour its obligations

- What financial means does the other side have? And how much does it have to lose?

- Whether the legal system will help or hinder those avenues

- Practicalities of the situation

- Commercial considerations beyond "who is right and who is wrong"

- What *isn't* written into the contract

That last point is worthy of particular and specific attention.

Engineering risk from a *liability* perspective

As any risk manager will tell you, the traditional focus of most risk engineering is on *assets*.

I would encourage you to expand and broaden that focus into the area of *liability*.

Risk engineering in the area of *liability* can be more difficult and inexact because we are not dealing with something tangible, as we are when looking at assets.

Instead, when it comes to contractual risk management, we are dealing with the conceptual.

It is important for you to try and understand the actual *concepts* contained within this *Commercial Contracts for Managers* Series.

- Some clauses may look similar, but may actually have different meanings.

- Conversely, clauses that may look completely different to ones you are familiar with, could actually have the same meaning.

Remember that traps don't carry warning signs or alarm bells – they are often hidden or disguised...

Reactive or proactive?

When dealing with contracts, it all comes down to whether your organisation wishes to be *reactive* or *proactive*. Take this simple test:

- Does your organisation focus on plugging holes *after* they have been seen and their effects have been felt? If your answer is 'yes', chances are that you work in to a *reactive* organisation.

- Does your company focus on finding holes *before* they leak and cause a disaster? If your answer is 'yes', chances are that you work in a *proactive* organisation.

Consider the example of how a pedestrian crossing the road might approach the process.

Reactive approach

A pedestrian about to cross the road:

- doesn't look each way;
- walks out onto the road;
- gets hit by a car;
- spares no expense in getting the very best medical care and therapy; and then
- keeps repeating the above steps until successful (or dead).

Proactive approach

By using a proactive approach the pedestrian:

- anticipates the dangers;
- forms an idea of what might happen if a car was to hit them; and then
- takes appropriate steps to mitigate the risk:
  - crosses at the lights;
  - looks for a break in traffic (even if it means having to wait for one)
  - looks both ways before crossing etc;
- lives to see another day.

It is a simple difference in execution, producing a drastic difference in outcome. This is the very essence of devising and implementing effective risk management strategies.

▌▌▌

A proactive mindset

The focus of this book is on organisations adopting a *proactive* mindset and attitude to contractual risk planning.

Golden Rule

In contract evaluation, preventative measures and safeguards are the best tools available.

Once you have committed to an unduly onerous contract that has not been properly scrutinised, it is often too late to renegotiate.

Remembering that you cannot 'unring' the proverbial bell.

So, should we just accept Conditions of Contract, without question?

How many times have you heard these old chestnuts from customers?

- *"Everyone else signs them without making any changes"*
- *"No-one else has ever objected to them"*
- *"You signed these same terms last year"*

Directors and managers certainly do not wish to be exposed to personal liability for having committed their company to a major loss-making contract or one that lacked basic and necessary safeguards. Worse still would be the case where valuable proprietary rights were actually surrendered or even *given* away.

Depending upon the gravity of such an unfortunate act or omission, it can be quite a career-limiting occurrence. To add insult to the injury of accusations of mismanagement, litigation could even potentially follow, from affected stakeholders.

Good corporate governance requires that corporations implement proactive programmes and strategies with emphasis on proper contract evaluation and scrutiny, at the front end, rather than having to overspend to fix a problem when one is in full 'damage control' mode, after the event.

These factors combine to make a fundamental understanding of contracts more relevant than ever.

▌▌▌

The cost of getting it wrong

In a worst-case scenario, accepting unduly onerous clauses in a contract could lead to:

- Losses of top-line revenue
- Loss of reputation in the marketplace

- Higher insurance premiums
- Increased audit or oversight requirements of parent company
- Litigation
- Increased operating costs
- The loss of any profit made in the transaction
- Loss of confidence of customers

It can become a downward and cyclical spiral.

Here are some "real life" examples I have advised upon (the circumstances have been changed to protect the guilty).

Bungle Number 1

- Invoice amount: €1,978.00

- Gross margin: €415.00

- **PROBLEM:** 500,000 litres of wine became mixed with 18,000 litres of brine – (salty wine isn't in especially high demand & also has a disposal cost - €!!)

- **RESULT:** Payout by company to the other party - €278,000.00

Bungle Number 2

- Company gave out some technical drawings and designs as a favour to help entice a prospective customer

- They actually purchased nothing from the Company. Therefore, the invoice amount was: Zero!

- **PROBLEM:** They claimed they relied on the drawings as advice and suffered a £300,000.00 loss.

- **RESULT:** Payout by company to the claimant - £80,000.00

Consider how much in top-line revenue sales is needed to generate the sums necessary to pay for the above bungles...

▌▐▐

Next steps

This book is divided into two separate sections:

1. **Part A** consists of the contract evaluation *micro* view – in this section we commence with an overview of the parts of a typical commercial agreement, as a brief refresher. We then proceed to dissect and consider some typically problematic contract clauses. The focus is on a number of different and significant contract clauses and issues that recur in everyday business exchanges. For example, some of the things we will look at are indemnities, liquidated damages, assignment and change of control clauses, *force majeure* and dispute resolution issues;

2. **Part B** consists of the *macro* view at a much higher level – where we take a step back and look at contract management from a macro perspective and compare the alternative ways that an organisation can deal with the flow of contracts and the competing evaluation models they can adopt – whether managing the flow of contracts should be handled centrally or whether it is best to have it decentralised. We will look at the arguments for and against each approach.

Chapter 2

PARTS OF A COMMERCIAL CONTRACT

▓▓▓

Recitals

Recitals set the background and help give some context to the transaction, which is the subject of the contract. It could also be said to be an executive summary of the nature, background and context of a contract (but generally not of the particular terms of the deal).

An example of the use of recitals is set out below. In this case, the recitals are from an agreement for the termination of an employee:

<u>WHEREAS</u> *On the _____ the parties entered into an agreement in which the Employer employed the Employee pursuant to the terms and* *conditions appearing therein ("the Agreement") and the parties now wish to terminate the said Agreement on the terms hereinafter set forth.*

In another example of the use of recitals, a confidentiality agreement produced by a vendor of a business (the "Discloser") and given to a prospective Buyer of that business (the "Recipient") might contain the following recitals:

Recitals

A) *The parties have entered into confidential discussions concerning a possible business relationship between them.*

B) *In order to facilitate such discussions the Recipient has requested the Discloser to disclose the Confidential Information to it solely and exclusively for the Permitted Purpose.*

C) *The Disclosers are in possession of the Confidential Information, which they wish to remain secret and confidential.*

D) *The Discloser has agreed to supply the Confidential Information to the Recipient on the condition that the Recipient enters into this Deed and complies with all of its obligations to protect the secret and confidential nature of that Confidential Information.*

Recitals may not appear underneath a heading "recitals", but may simply appear at the beginning of a document after the word "Whereas" or, in some cases, the word "Background" is being used with increasing frequency, where modern language drafting is used. There is no difference in either method as its use is merely a matter of personal preference.

The use of recitals is not mandatory but tends to be customary in most jurisdictions. An archaic custom is to only use capital letters to mark recitals (Recital A, B, C etc), rather than numbers (1, 2, 3 etc). The advent of plain-English drafting has seen the virtual disappearance of this practice.

One should strive to be concise and exercise the same care in their drafting, as one would for the substantive provisions of a document.

Their significance

Collaborative bargaining tends to accentuate the common ground existing between the parties and to look for the shared interest. The focus is centred upon *interests*, rather than traditional *positions*.

When it comes to drafting the contract, these interests can sometimes be set out in the contract, as *recitals*.

By setting the background to the transaction, *recitals* give some context to the subject and purpose of the contract. It can be a convenient way of recording the parties' intentions, which could become valuable interpretation tools for a court in the event of a dispute.

Recitals are not an operative part of the contract. However, a court will consider them (if relevant) in deciding upon an interpretation of a particular part of the contract in dispute.

In some jurisdictions, a court may consider them to be evidence of representations or warranties made, the breach of which may give rise to an action by the party asserting their reliance upon them.

A lawyer in the relevant jurisdiction should be consulted to advise you on the best way to deal with recitals in your particular transaction.

Definitions

The *definitions* section defines certain specific terms in the agreement. It should be contained in the operative part of the agreement and not with the recitals. This is because the definitions section defines terms that actually form part of the agreement.

Capitalised terms in an agreement (aside from proper names) are usually a prompt for the reader to refer to the definitions section for a full definition of the term.

For example, in the recitals shown above, you will note that Confidential Information, Permitted Purpose and Discloser and Recipient are capitalised terms, which means that they are more fully defined elsewhere in the agreement.

In a simple agreement it is best to define the term as it appears. Whereas, in a more complex and detailed agreement, it is best to group all of the definitions into a "definitions" section of the agreement.

A definition should be expressed simply in a way that leaves no room for misinterpretation:

In this Agreement X shall mean and include Y.

[X being the term to be defined]

[Y being the actual definition of that term]

> *Golden Nugget*
>
> # Limiting definitions
>
> Only using the word "means" in a definition can potentially limit it to the words used – and no others.
>
> For example:
>
> Contrast:
>
> *"**Force Majeure Event**" means storm, tempest, terrorism, war, civil unrest, insurrection or riot.*
>
> With the broader:
>
> *"**Force Majeure Event**" means <u>and includes</u> storm, tempest, terrorism, war, civil unrest, insurrection or riot.*
>
> When one uses the words "means and includes" in a definition, it does not close off the definition to anything else that may be relevant.

For convenience, it is common to also see general interpretation clauses in a specific definition section of a contract. For example:

In this Agreement the use of the singular number shall include the plural and vice versa, and the use of any gender shall include all other genders.

> ### Golden Nugget
>
> Be on the alert for "sneaky" definitions.
>
> For example, assume in a contract that the full definition of "Loss" includes consequential and indirect losses.
>
> However, if you do not carefully read and understand the definition section, you only see the word "Loss" when reading the contract, thereby gaining no understanding of what it actually means and includes.

▌▐▐

Substantive clauses

The *substantive* part of the contract document is usually preceded by the following form of words:

Now it is hereby agreed as follows:

OR the more archaic form

Now this deed witnesseth:

There are two categories of substantive clauses:

- **deal terms;** and
- **boilerplate.**

"Deal" terms

Deal terms are what the contract is all about. These are the terms of the commercial deal to which the parties have come together and agreed.

Deal terms will typically detail:

- what one party will do for the other — that is, supply certain goods and/or perform certain services;

- the *term* of the agreement. For example, whether the agreement is for a term of one year with an option to renew, for three years with no option to renew, etc;

- the time limits within which such goods must be supplied or such services must be performed;

- the specifications which the supplier must meet and standards to which the goods and/or the services must adhere or conform;

- what is to happen in the event that such time limits, specifications or standards are not met; and

- the agreed price to be paid for the fulfilment of the supply side of the contract as well as the timing for payment and any mechanism for the adjustment of the price, if necessary.

These terms are peculiar to each deal and reflect the parties' agreement for that particular transaction. That is, the deal terms will typically reflect the bargain the parties have agreed to and "shaken hands" upon.

"Boilerplate" clauses

The commercial or deal terms of the contract tend to receive the most careful scrutiny within an organisation, with the rest (eg, *boilerplate* clauses) being largely left "for the lawyers to sort out". Because boilerplate clauses tend to be added or produced at the end of contract negotiations, they often receive scant attention.

However, boilerplate clauses play a pivotal part in a contract, as it is the boilerplate clauses that govern or regulate the other commercial or deal terms.

Accordingly, given their significance, this book is dedicated to and focuses on boilerplate clauses.

▒▒▒

Warranties

A *warranty* is an assurance or promise in a contract. It usually relates to assurances about past or present facts in the particular transaction, the subject of the contract.

For example, an agreement for the sale of a business might contain the following assurance or warranty:

The business has no outstanding tax liabilities.

No matter how good a party's due diligence, other "intelligence gathering" or background investigations, it cannot expect to find out *everything* about a particular transaction before entering into it. The parties will agree on price and terms based upon their actual knowledge and on the strength of the representations made by the other — typically, at the time of entering into the contract.

The purpose of the warranty is to give the recipient of that warranty the right to sue for damages, if such assurance later proves untrue or inaccurate.

Golden Nugget

Limits and restrictions in warranties

It is common practice for warranties in a transaction such as the sale of a business to be subject to certain <u>limits</u> or <u>thresholds</u>.

However, there are exceptions to this principle:

A) in the case of tax warranties; and

B) to the extent that any claim arises by reason of any fraud or willful misstatement or omission by the vendor.

The thresholds or limits of warranties in a transaction such as the sale of a business are typically the following:

- *the vendor is usually under no obligation to make any payment for breach of warranty unless the amount of any single claim exceeds a certain monetary value;*

- *the vendor is usually under no obligation to make payment for breach of warranty unless the* aggregate liability *in respect of* all *warranty claims is in excess of a certain monetary value;*

- *the aggregate liability of the vendor in respect of all warranty claims is typically limited to the sale price; and*

> - *there is a time limit within which any claims for breach of warranty must be notified in writing to the vendor. Usually, the time limit is expressed to be within a certain number of months from the date of the agreement.*

The breach of a warranty gives rise to a claim for damages. Such damages, if awarded, are subject to the common law rules relating to the assessment of damages. For example, damages will be subject to the test of remoteness, the duty to mitigate the loss etc.

The ultimate effect of such common law rules is that the recipient of the warranty may recover *substantially* less than all losses connected with the breach.

A properly worded and well-worded indemnity, instead, can make the *entire* loss recoverable.

For a more in-depth treatment of indemnity clauses as well seeing detailed examples, you should consult *The Managers Guide to Understanding Indemnity Clauses*, the first volume in the *Commercial Contracts for Managers Series*.

> ### *Golden Nugget*
> # Subtle distinctions in warranties
>
> Note there is a subtle, but distinct, difference between an *absolute* warranty and one based on *knowledge*.
>
> For example,
>
> *There are no court proceedings against the Company* – **[this is an absolute warranty]**
>
> **AND**
>
> <u>*As far as the vendor is aware*</u> *there are no court proceedings against the*
>
> *Company* – **[this is a far less onerous warranty, as it is based only knowledge]**

Execution clauses

The *execution* clause is the section signed by the parties. It is usually preceded by wording "introducing" the signatures as follows:

IN WITNESS WHEREOF, the parties hereto have caused their duly authorised representatives to execute this Agreement as at the date first above written.

OR

using a slightly more archaic form of wording:

> *IN WITNESS WHEREOF the parties hereto have hereunto affixed their hands and seals on the day and year first hereinbefore written.*

The execution sections themselves sometimes appear as follows.

For individuals

For ordinary contracts:

> *Signed by the said John Smith in the presence of:*

> _____

> *Witness*

For contracts under seal:

> *Signed sealed and delivered by the said John Smith in the presence of:*

> _____

> *Witness*

For corporations

For ordinary contracts:

> *Signed for and behalf of XYZ Limited by:*

_____

OR

> *Signed for and behalf of XYZ Limited by*
>
> *its duly authorised representative:*

_____

For contracts under seal:

> *The Common Seal of XYZ*
> *Limited was hereunto*
> *affixed by authority of the*
> *board of directors in the*
> *presence of:*

_____   _____

Director   *Secretary*

The relevant companies legislation in each jurisdiction prescribes the correct manner and form for a company to execute documents. In Australia, for example, section 127(1) of the Corporations Act prescribes that documents executed by a company need not have a company seal affixed, but shall be signed by either two directors, or, a director and the company secretary. For single director companies, the signature of that director alone is sufficient.

In Australia, the law entitles one to assume that a document has been properly executed by the company if done in the manner described.

In New Zealand, section 180 of the Companies Act 1993 ("Act") deals with the method of contracting for companies in New Zealand. Essentially, a deed must be entered into by two or more directors of the company or, if there is only one director, by that director whose signature must be witnessed. The constitution of the company can modify this. For example, the Act provides that if a company's constitution so provides, a director or other person or class of person may execute a deed and their signature must be witnessed.

In the USA, generally only one signature is required provided the person has been authorised by the company to execute documents on its behalf. One typically asks for the company's secretary (or assistant secretary) to certify that a person who is signing a document is authorised to do so.

Execution under power of attorney

Where a document is executed under a power of attorney, the *donor* or *grantor* (the company granting the authority under the power of attorney) delegates a specific person/s (called the *donee* or *grantee*) with the relevant authority of the Board of Directors, to execute a document on behalf of the company.

The following matters are key:

1. That the original of the power of attorney is sighted;

2. Sometimes, it might be appropriate to ask for a copy of the Directors' resolutions to be produced – for example, in the case of a financing agreement, a lending bank would almost certainly require a borrower company to produce these;

3. The execution clause should contain a statement to the effect that the *donee* of the power of attorney (the person being empowered to sign on behalf of the company) is not aware of the power of attorney having been revoked – and actually makes a positive statement to not having received any notice of revocation;

4. Check whether local law requires a power of attorney to be *stamped* – that is, where the document attracts a duty of some kind, that duty may have to be paid before the document gains validity;

5. Check whether local law requires a power of attorney to be registered with a governmental authority before it is valid (sometimes, stamp duty may have

to be paid on the document before it can be actually registered) – for example, where the power of attorney is used to authorise the *donee* to execute a contract for the sale or purchase of land on behalf of the *donor*. If so, do a search to ensure that it actually has been registered.

Counterparts clause

A useful clause to use when dealing with execution of documents is the *counterparts* clause.

Normally, *all* parties should sign *all* copies of the agreement.

However, this is sometimes not possible when there are tight deadlines and the parties may be separated by distance. For example, an American company may be entering into an agreement with a Japanese company to purchase a business situated in Germany. In this case, lawyers in Germany may be preparing the contract and signatures are required in Germany as well as in the USA and Japan by the respective parent companies of both the Buyer and vendor, in anticipation of completion.

In this case, there may not be time available for all copies of the documents to travel the globe for signature. In that case, a counterparts clause is a useful tool to help shorten the process and ultimately achieve the same result. Such a clause may read as follows:

COUNTERPARTS

This Agreement may be executed in any number of counterparts (including by facsimile) and by the parties to it on separate counterparts, each of which is an original but all of which together constitute one and the same instrument.

Golden Nugget

The difference between "ordinary" contracts and contracts "under seal"

Ordinary contracts are sometimes referred to as documents executed "under hand", as opposed to being executed "under seal".

As a brief reminder, ordinary contracts require the following essential elements to be binding agreements:

1. offer;

2. acceptance;

3. consideration; and

4. intention to create legal relations.

Executing a document as a *deed* (often referred to as executing a document *under seal*) eliminates the requirement for *consideration*, number 3 on our list above.

Note that in Australia, for example, the actual affixing of a seal is no longer a requirement for the execution of a deed.

In some common law jurisdictions (for example, in England), executing a document as a deed has the effect of extending the statute of limitation period under which a claim can be made from six years to 12.

That has also been the case in New South Wales (Australia) since 1971. However, this difference has been mainly eroded by unfair contracts or contracts review legislation enacted over the last 25 years. Such an erosion of the practical difference between ordinary contracts and contracts under seal has also occurred in a number of other jurisdictions.

Headings

Headings to clauses and sections serve as a convenience and as an aid to reading. To have them forming part of the contract can over-complicate any question of interpretation of a particular section or sections.

Prudent drafting should always include a clause to the effect that:

The headings in this Agreement are for ease of reference only and shall not be considered in the construction or interpretation of any provision hereof.

OR

Headings are for convenience only and do not affect interpretation.

Schedules

Schedules should always be expressly incorporated as a substantive part of a contract.

Their purpose is to separate much of the deal-specific detail from the boilerplate sections. They are much-used in standard form agreements. Any deal-specific tailoring of the agreement is then done in the schedules.

They usually contain things such as:

1. product and/or service specifications;

2. key performance indicators;

3. warranties;

4. disclosure items;

5. asset lists or registers;

6. lists of employees; and

7. any forms the parties will need to use between one another during the course of the transaction.

Disclosure letter

A *disclosure letter* is most commonly used as a schedule to an agreement for the sale of a business or company. Its purpose is to make disclosures against the warranties contained within the main body of the contract.

Such sale agreements often contemplate that a Seller will disclose to the Buyer certain matters that would (or could) otherwise give rise to a claim under the warranties – in other words, the disclosure introduces a threshold, against which a Buyer cannot make a claim under the warranties.

The effect of this disclosure is that the Buyer will be unable to use any of the disclosed matters as the basis for a claim under the warranties.

The disclosure letter is usually the subject of intense negotiations.

Chapter 3

THE "TOP 20" CONTRACT PROVISIONS

▓▓▓

This chapter is where the "rubber meets the road".

This is where we dissect and consider the "Top 20" contract provisions that frequently cause the most grief. They appear in no particular order – but they are all significant contributors of risk to the recipient of such clauses.

What we endeavour to do here is to flag some of the more common tricks and loopholes to be aware of when reviewing such clauses.

Capital expenditure (CAPEX)

Certain types of contracts will demand a certain investment of capital by a service provider.

CAPEX is expenditure that will usually appear as a *fixed asset* in the service provider's own financial accounts.

Before submitting a CAPEX proposal to a potential customer, most organisations will have a number of internal thresholds to meet and a certain defined processes to follow.

For example,

- there may be specific limits of expenditure that can be approved at a local level, without requiring regional or even head office approval.

- Many organisations will also have specific *return on capital employed* (ROCE) hurdles to be met to gain internal approval for CAPEX authorisation. A business case for CAPEX approval may be required to demonstrate an expected ROCE of somewhere around 15%-20% (this depends upon the individual corporate benchmarks, such as the organisation's borrowing costs, as well as the industry itself).

Whilst most businesses will be prepared to spend money to make money (within reasonable limits), they will want to see their investment protected, especially in the event of an early termination of the contract. In that case it would require the other party to agree to some kind of automatic buy-back provision, at a predetermined and pre-agreed value; for example, the book value of the assets.

CAPEX checklist

☑ Is the amount within the Manager's normal limits of authority?

☑ Are there specific return on capital employed (ROCE) requirements to be met? In many organisations the ROCE requirement is usually about 15-20%.

☑ Is the CAPEX amount able to be amortised over the life of the contract?

☑ Is the CAPEX amount properly protected under the contract in the case of early termination for whatever reason?

☑ Has a business case for the CAPEX required been prepared?

☑ Has it been approved (if necessary)?

☑ At the end of the Contract term, is there a compulsory buy-back provision in the contract for the Buyer, or the incoming Contractor?

███

Pricing

It is normally prudent to do all things possible to ensure that contract pricing is not fixed for the entire term of the contract (unless there are valid reasons for actually doing this), without an appropriate allowance for "rise and fall".

The costs of supplies/materials may fluctuate during the currency of the contract. To reflect this, an appropriate allowance should be made in the contract for such "rise and fall". Rise and fall clauses in contracts are also used to adjust the wage component of contract costs in line with movements in the cost of labour.

On occasion, a contract may provide for a periodic price review to be determined "by agreement" of the parties. Where the parties are deadlocked on the issue or fall into dispute because they cannot agree on a regime for pricing review, the ideal contractual position for the Seller might be to be able to terminate the contract without penalty and "walk away". Obviously, such a proposal could be expected to meet with some degree of resistance from a Buyer, who may far prefer a dispute resolution mechanism to be triggered in the event of a failure to agree, rather than an automatic termination of the contract.

A Seller will want to ensure that there is sufficient provision in the contract enabling it to pass on to the Buyer any Value Added Taxes (VAT), *as well as* making allowance for any other taxes or levies that are or may be imposed in the future.

Pricing Checklist

☑ Is pricing fixed?

☑ Is there allowance for a periodic increase (say, every year)?

☑ If so, is there a specified rate or agreed formula for the increase? Or is it to be determined by negotiation? What happens if there is no agreement reached? Can we withdraw from the contract without penalty? Is there a defined dispute resolution mechanism, setting out the steps to be followed? How much time will it take to go through such a procedure? Must we continue working during this time or can we "down tools"?

☑ Has there been a proper allowance made for "rise and fall" in pricing? For labour and materials, as well as profit?

☑ Is the scope of any potential variations sufficiently restricted to areas of contract services or expertise of the provider? Are the variations optional for the service provider to carry out, or are they mandatory? Is there a model or procedure to follow for pricing of variations?

☑ Is there a model or procedure to follow for pricing on an extension or renewal of the agreement after contract expiry?

☑ Are we able to pass on the additional costs of any tax such as any Value Added Taxes (VAT)?

☑ Can we pass on any increases in current taxes or any new taxes that might be imposed in the future?

Pricing options/methods available to a Seller

Often, the risk profile of a transaction can be completely altered by changing the structure of the transaction – i.e. changing or refining the pricing method or business model of the transaction.

Such a change could turn an unattractive and uneconomic transaction into a profitable and rewarding one, and vice-versa.

1.   **Input Charging**
     Service/product costs plus the Seller's margin

2.   **Output Charging**
     Based on a detailed understanding of each service outputs which there is an agreed unit price

3.   **Risk/Reward Based Charging**
     To reflect the Seller's value added to the customer's business and the value of the risk accepted by the Seller

▓▓▓

Variations to the scope of works or specifications

The fact is that many contracts actually evolve from the beginnings of a handshake and signed document.

A part of this contractual evolution is the process of variations to the contract.

So what happens when parties agree to vary or amend the contract? Do they simply take each other's word for it? Or, do they need to agree on specific amended wording to the existing contract?

Note that in many instances, the boilerplate part of the contract rarely needs altering. Such terms usually do not require any kind of change. Variations tend to occur in the Scope of works or specification section of the contract.

In that case, before entering into the contract, we need to run through the following checklists, concerning that scope of works:

SCOPE OF WORKS CHECKLIST

☑ Is it clearly defined?

☑ Is it properly documented?

☑ Is it unequivocal or is there room for interpretation on the main issues?

☑ Can it be properly priced in its current form?

How are *variations* to the scope of works dealt with?

- Does the contract permit unilateral variations to the scope of the works?

- Is the acceptance of those unilateral variations *mandatory* for the other party?

- Is the process of requiring variations clearly defined?

- Is the *scope* within which variations can be made, properly defined and delineated?

- How is the pricing of any variations to be determined? By reference to an already agreed formula? Or, by agreement? What happens if the parties are unable to agree?

It goes without saying that any kind of variation or change to a contract should be properly documented

It is not enough for one party to say:

"We will agree to vary the price upwards".

Such a statement leaves many things in doubt:

- Under what circumstances will the price be increased?

- By how much?

- On what terms?

- Who decides by how much?

Golden Rule

It is important to realise that, under some circumstances, conduct by the parties (that is inconsistent with, or different to, the written terms of the contract), can have the effect of actually amending the contract.

Implied Terms

The issue of variations provides a useful lead-in to the topic of implied terms in a contract. One needs to be sensitive to the issue of implied terms - even if the parties have not mentioned a term in a contract, a court is able to imply such a term. It does so by considering custom, common law or statute.

Consider the following example,

- I purchase an object that falls apart or fails the next day

- There was nothing in the contract that stated it was in good condition

Such a term would be implied into the sale contract by Consumer Sale of Goods or Trade Practices legislation (or variations thereof) existing in most jurisdictions.

Depending upon the jurisdiction, any term *implied* into a contract by the court must usually be:

1) reasonable and equitable;

2) necessary – without which the contract would be ineffective;

3) so obvious that it "goes without saying";

4) capable of clear expression; and

5) must not contradict any express term of the contract.

The crucial elements to be aware of with respect to implied terms are:

1. Don't enter into a contract that you know is silent on vital terms, hoping that a court will imply those into the agreement;

2. However, do be aware of the prospect of the other party to the contract being able to ask a court to imply such terms in a contract, that might operate in their favour against you.

Understand that any time you are considering having a court implying terms into a contract, your focus shifts from resolution of a dispute, to litigation.

Disputes and alternative dispute resolution (ADR)

Once signed, contract documents tend only to be referred to when the parties are in dispute and relationships between parties deteriorate. By the time the "gloves come off", the lines of communication become severely strained or even severed. By this stage, logic and reason are not at their peak.

Once the parties consult their lawyers, there is a risk that the advice they receive will be restricted to the wording of the contract document, sometimes in isolation of the background and context of the dispute.

Disputes can end up following one of three possible paths (in order of escalating magnitude, cost, aggravation and damage to commercial relationships):

1. resolution between the parties, without external assistance;

2. some form of alternative dispute resolution (ADR);

3. they proceed to litigation.

Each of the three methods above will produce a result. However, the consequences and eventual "fallout" will differ considerably between the three methods.

The first method, *resolution between the parties:* is obviously the preferred one in terms of low-cost, low aggravation and the maintenance of business relationships. The parties have a much better chance of being able to continue to work together in harmony after the dispute is resolved.

The second method, *ADR:* has gained much favour with organisations in recent times. This is because it often represents the best compromise between the three methods available. In theory, it retains most of the benefits of the first method, whilst eliminating most of the disadvantages of litigation.

The third method, *litigation:* differs from the first two methods in that a solution is ultimately *imposed* upon the parties. Also, the disadvantages of higher costs and drain on management time are significant factors. Furthermore, the element of confidentiality is lost. The dispute and all the evidence presented becomes a matter of public record. Press headlines concerning litigation ultimately do no favours for either litigant, even for the winner. This is because the focus will tend be on highlighting the shortcomings of both parties. Rarely is one party completely and totally "in the right" and blameless. There generally tends to be "dirty laundry" on both sides. The "dirty laundry" of one party will almost certainly receive an airing by the opposing party (sometimes – but not always – the best form of defence is attack).

The timeframes of litigation are measured in years. The costs can be horrendous, sometimes even out of proportion to the scale of the original dispute. The parties are rarely able to continue working together after litigation. For these reasons, litigation is and should always be, the method of last recourse in a commercial situation.

Our focus, for the purpose of this topic, is ADR.

ADR methods

Methods other than traditional litigation in courts are becoming increasingly popular, particularly as they can provide solutions more quickly and at lower costs.

ADR methods tend to have the benefits of confidentiality and informality. Everything that is said or disclosed is not a matter of public record as it would be in most traditional courts.

Also the savings in legal costs can sometimes be considerable. However, such cost savings can be negated in the instance where an arbitration hearing is appealed by referring the matter to a court for a rehearing before a judge.

Also, on the question of costs, one must remember that expenses such as:

- the hiring of rooms;

- stenographers and/or recording equipment (to create a transcript of the proceedings);

- the Arbitrator/s' fees;

must be paid for by the participants. The cost savings can sometimes be less than first thought.

One of the primary benefits of ADR is speed. This is often a significant point to be considered, especially in relation to a long term contract, where the outcome can affect the parties significantly in the future.

The most often-used methods of ADR in escalating order are:

1. Good faith negotiations between the chief executive officers of each party and (in some circumstances) a lawyer.

2. Mediation, which is becoming a more popular method. This involves the use of an independent and impartial mediator whose role is to encourage the parties to find positive ways of resolving their differences in an amicable and non-confrontational way. The mediator does not provide a binding decision at the end of the mediation but if the final settlement terms arrived at are acceptable, the parties can agree to be bound by them.

3. Arbitration is almost akin to a private and slightly less formal trial. Procedure and rules of evidence are generally adhered to in arbitration proceedings.

An arbitrator is appointed who (similarly to a judge in a court) hears the evidence, rules on objections during the hearing and will make findings of fact and issue a decision on the dispute. Depending upon the jurisdiction, there may be:

- a right to have the matter reheard in court;
- a limited right of appeal to a court; or
- a prohibition on any appeal or rehearing of the matter in a court.

Parties can agree to use any one of these methods to deal with a dispute, or a combination of methods. For example, before resorting to litigation, a contract might provide that the parties first enter into negotiations between the chief executive officers of the respective parties. If that proves unsuccessful, the next step may generally be to have the matter mediated and so on.

There may be a provision in a contract preventing recourse to a court before exhausting all of the prescribed ADR remedies. A wise qualification to make to such a clause is an exception for "urgent interlocutory applications".

One of the difficulties with ADR is that the methods may not always be as final and conclusive as they are in traditional courts. It is important to also be aware that an arbitration award obtained in one jurisdiction may not be enforceable in certain other jurisdictions. This consideration is particularly relevant where the other party is a foreign entity. Also with noting in many common law jurisdictions, is the developing body of case-law dealing with parties attempting to oust the jurisdiction of the courts.

The use of ADR methods can be provided for in a contract by including an appropriate ADR clause. Dispute resolution clauses generally require use of ADR as either a precursor or alternative to arbitration or litigation. In a number of countries, there are various dispute resolution centres or agencies that are able to provide commercial mediators. These organisations often provide their own preferred boilerplate mediation and ADR clauses.

You should ensure that you seek advice from a qualified lawyer in the appropriate jurisdiction/s applicable to your contract, before consenting to the inclusion of ADR clauses in a contract, particularly where such clauses attempt to usurp or otherwise oust the jurisdiction of the courts.

Golden Nugget

Place strict time limits on ADR procedures, especially where court proceedings must be deferred until after the prescribed ADR avenues have been exhausted.

The absence of time limits could prolong "good faith negotiations between the parties" indefinitely.

▌▌▌

Joint and several liability clause

A joint and several liability clause might look something like this:

> *In this Agreement, all covenants, agreements, undertakings, representations, warranties and indemnities by more than one person are given jointly and severally.*

Firstly, it is necessary to understand what is meant by the term *joint and several liability*. This term often appears in contracts where there are two or more persons (or companies) as one party to a contract.

For example, assume the parties to a contract are **Terry Towling** and **Anne Attomee** (the "**Tenants**"), entering into a property lease with **Slumworld PLC** (the "**Landlord**").

Also, assume the contract provides that:

> *The **Tenants** shall be <u>jointly and severally liable</u> to the **Landlord**.*

In the event of default by *either or both* **Terry** and **Anne**, the **Landlord** would be entitled to sue <u>either or both</u> **Terry** and **Anne**. The **Landlord** would not need to commence proceedings against them separately or individually.

The **Landlord** could elect to sue *only* **Terry** to recover its loss, if say, **Anne** had disappeared or gone bankrupt.

It would then be entirely up to **Terry** to attempt to sue **Anne** to seek contribution from her, to apportion the loss evenly between them.

A common area of usage of such a provision is in banking documentation. When there are two or more co-borrowers, the bank's loan documentation will always contain a joint and several liability provision, covering any default of any one borrower or all of the borrowers.

Key Issues

When evaluating a contract containing such a clause against you, you need to carefully consider:

- How similar are the interests of the parties, who are joint and severally liable?
  - o For example, does one party only hold a 50% stake in the outcome and in return face a potential 100% risk?

- What are the respective <u>means</u> of each party to become jointly and severally liable?
  - o This refers to the *actual* means, rather than the *apparent* ones. For example, there are many subsidiary companies of large household-name groups of companies that may be technically

insolvent. The only way they maintain solvency is with parent company support. If that support stops, the subsidiary "dies" (along with your prospects of seeking any contribution for their share).

- How stable are the other parties?
  - o Take heed of the favourite statement used in the securities and investment industry:

"Past performance is no indicator or guarantee of future returns".

Golden Rule

You should *never* agree to accept joint and several liability with another party (or parties), unless you are fully prepared to assume 100% of the liability.

Limitations of the clause

In the event that the roles are reversed and you are the one requiring two or more other parties to be jointly and severally liable to you, it would be prudent to have a clause containing express wording enabling you to release any of the others from liability, without affecting the liability to you of the remainder.

In the case of a loan agreement, such a clause might read as follows:

The Lender may release settle or compromise, in whole or in part, the liability of any one or more borrowers or may grant an extension of time or other indulgence to one or more Borrowers without affecting the liability of the other Borrowers.

In the absence of such express wording, any settlement or compromise with one of the parties liable to you, could, in some jurisdictions, have the unintended (and highly undesirable) side effect of releasing *all* parties from any liability to you.

Indemnities

More often than not, the party acquiring a product or service ("Buyer") will require a prospective provider of those goods or services ("Seller") to give an indemnity for any loss sustained by the Buyer, in the event of any breach of the contract by the Seller.

An indemnity is a contractual commitment by a party to make good a specified loss suffered by the other party. In other words, it is an acknowledgment and promise by one party to cover the potential liability of another.

Such a clause might typically read as follows:

The Seller shall indemnify and hold harmless the Buyer (including but not limited to the Buyer's officers, employees, contractors and agents) against all losses, damages, costs or expenses which the Buyer incurs or may incur as a result of any act, omission, negligence or breach of this Agreement by the Seller.

Notice the clause above does not contain restrictions or limits upon:

1. the types of losses sustained by the Buyer;

2. whether the obligation to indemnify is limited only to direct losses sustained by the Buyer;

3. whether the obligation to indemnify extends to include indirect (or consequential) losses or otherwise;

4. whether the obligation to indemnify arises only through the actions or inactions of the Seller, or in combination with those of a third party.

Golden Nugget

Burn this concept into your memory...

The extent of liability under an indemnity does not depend on the dollar value of the contract.

Key Issues

- A key feature of an indemnity is that the obligation created by it can often extend *beyond* that which would otherwise be imposed on a party under the general law.

- Typically, in a claim for a breach of contract, the party seeking to recover its loss might not recover *all* of the loss incurred. The indemnity, however, will extend to cover losses that might not otherwise have been covered by a claim for damages for breach of the agreement. That is to say, in the event of a successfully proven breach in a court of law, the damages bill will generally be higher with an indemnity clause than without one.

- An indemnity is a particularly attractive mechanism to outsource liability to the other party to the contract. This is because its very concept is to make the injured party whole again, as if the loss had not occurred, *even if the person who agrees to indemnify would not otherwise have had any obligation to do so.*

Indemnity Checklist:

When evaluating an indemnity clause, typically the main issues to focus upon are:

1) Liability extends well beyond the terms of the contract, or, even for negligence alone.

2) There is no exception for the acts, omissions or negligence of <u>third parties</u> not under the direct control of the party giving the indemnity.

3) There is no exception for the acts, omissions or negligence of <u>the other party</u> to the contract.

4) There is no reduction in liability <u>to the extent</u> of negligence. (i.e. an equitable apportionment of responsibility where more than one party has contributed to the loss)

5) Where one party expressly agrees to accept responsibility for the acts of third parties over which they do not exercise control

6) Clauses where a <u>joint</u> or even <u>partial</u> contribution of liability from another source can *extinguish* a party's obligation to indemnify

7) There is no specific and <u>express exclusion</u> for consequential or indirect loss or damage.

8) Whether liability is otherwise restricted, limited or capped in any way.

Given their significance, it is vitally important to have a lawyer carefully check indemnity clauses in a contract.

For a more comprehensive discussion on indemnity clauses and a demonstration of specific examples of the use of such clauses, you should consult *The Managers Guide to Understanding Indemnity Clauses*, the first volume in the *Commercial Contracts for Managers Series*.

Consequential loss

To reiterate, an equitably balanced indemnity clause does not seek to avoid a party's responsibility or liability for its actions. It merely seeks to limit the extent of liability to that which may be *directly* attributable to any negligence or wrongdoing.

It can be argued that consequential loss clauses are not normal or reasonable commercial terms. Normal loss is the loss suffered as a *direct* result of a breach or action. Whereas, consequential loss is the loss suffered because of *circumstances peculiar to a particular person or entity*.

It can, therefore, be argued that a clause allowing consequential damages to be claimed *would unfairly broaden and extend liability beyond the normal commercial realm*.

Consequential losses, by their nature, are uncertain and difficult to quantify. They involve the acceptance of responsibility for risks that are not foreseeable and not within the ordinary knowledge of the party giving the indemnity. In addition, they can in some circumstances even extend to include the losses of persons who are not parties to the agreement!

As with all things in the law, often the choices are not only restricted to either black or white. Compromise is an essential feature of successful negotiations over commercial contracts.

The choice confronting a party to a commercial contract might often be either to accept a consequential loss clause or not.

Alternatively, where a party has specific concerns relating to a *particular* event of consequential loss, it may be possible for the parties to direct their minds to dealing specifically and only with such an event, to attempt to find a mutually acceptable solution to the problem.

Key Issues

- Consequential losses (sometimes referred to as indirect losses), by their nature are uncertain and difficult to quantify. They involve the acceptance of responsibility for risks that are *not within the ordinary knowledge of the party giving the indemnity*

- Direct loss is the loss suffered as a *direct* result of a breach or action.

  It is an **objective** measure

- Whereas, consequential loss is the loss suffered because of *circumstances peculiar to a particular person or entity*.

  It is a **subjective** measure

Strategies to deal with consequential loss

1. Avoid it – *reject the clause*. **This is corporate policy at many companies**

2. If you must accept it, then try to *limit it to a specific event/s*

3. If you can, then try to *limit the amount* (by using a liability ceiling or cap)

In any event, you must ensure that you <u>always</u> have appropriate and sufficient insurance cover.

For a more comprehensive discussion on consequential loss, you should consult *The Managers Guide to Understanding Indemnity Clauses*, the first volume in the *Commercial Contracts for Managers Series*.

Liquidated damages

On occasion, a Buyer will require a Seller to agree to a liquidated damages clause in a contract.

This enables a Buyer to place on record a genuine pre-estimate of the amount of damages or loss that it will suffer in the event of a breach by the Seller (it can be a stated dollar amount or an amount easily ascertainable by reference to a fixed scale of charges or by a simple calculation).

The estimate must be within certain limits and not "out of all proportion".

It is designed to overcome the necessity for a Buyer to otherwise have to prove loss in a claim for damages. By doing so, it can save the Buyer time and make the recovery proceedings considerably less expensive for a Buyer.

The provision is becoming increasingly common in service contracts.

If the agreed figure is not a genuine pre-estimate of the loss, it may be construed by a court to be a penalty – in a number of common law jurisdictions, penalties are regarded as being contrary to public policy and therefore unenforceable. As this is a developing area of the law, you should check with your lawyer to establish the correct position for your particular jurisdiction.

The generally accepted test of whether a liquidated damages claim amounts to a penalty is whether the amount claimed is "extravagant and unconscionable".

The fact that it may be merely "unfair" may not be sufficient to move a court to strike such a clause down, as the parties will be required to stand by their bargain.

Prudent practice (from a Seller's perspective) requires that some form of *ceiling* or *cap* be placed on any total liquidated damages amount claimed by a Buyer.

What should you do when confronted with a request for the inclusion in a contract of a liquidated damages clause?

- Either reject such a clause (if you are able to)

OR

- Place some form of *ceiling* or *cap* on any total liquidated damages amount claimed by the other party.

Normal acceptance tolerances for liquidated damages can vary between organisations. As a guide, one household name multinational has a rule of accepting liquidated damages capped at 0.5% per week up to a maximum of 5% in the aggregate.

> ### *Golden Rule*
>
> Generally, a capped liquidated damages provision is preferable to accepting a blanket time of the essence obligation.

▓▓▓

Ownership of intellectual property

Often, a Seller will "bring to the table" some form of proprietary information, product or other expertise. A particular product or skill-set can actually be one of the prime reasons behind the Seller's ultimate selection by a Buyer. This category of intellectual property rights may be referred to as *background intellectual property rights*.

Whereas, the intellectual property rights created during the course of a contract are sometimes referred to as *foreground intellectual property rights*.

A Seller will generally seek to retain *both* categories of rights.

It will depend upon the particular circumstances of the situation whether:

- the Buyer is paying the Seller only for some *limited right to use* such proprietary information; or

- the Buyer is paying the Seller to actually devise or develop such proprietary information for the Buyer's exclusive use and ownership.

This is a crucial point to bear in mind. It is something that must be absolutely clear and unequivocal in the contract documentation.

Depending upon the circumstances, the Buyer's contract documents may contain provisions either granting the Buyer the exclusive ownership of the intellectual property developed by the Seller or perhaps only granting some form of limited permission for its use.

Intellectual Property (IP) Infringement

When dealing with any kind of IP ownership issues, it is common (and not unreasonable) for a Buyer to seek protection (usually in the form of an indemnity clause) against claims by any third party that:

- the IP claimed to be owned by the Seller infringes some right of the third party; and/or

- the use of such IP by the Buyer constitutes an infringement of such third party's rights.

To avoid the likelihood of such cases occurring, the Buyer needs to verify the Seller's clear ownership and title to the items that the Buyer is contracting for the Seller to supply.

In the current climate, a new wave of what is colloquially referred to as "patent trolling" has taken hold in the USA, which has consequently produced a sharp increase in intellectual property claims and litigation. The term refers to those owners of a patent right who aggressively (and some would say opportunistically) enforce those rights against alleged infringers of those patents – the pejorative nature of the term "trolls" arises from the fact that the patent holder rarely manufactures or commercialises the patented invention. There are a number of companies emerging whose sole business model is the acquisition and enforcement of patent rights.

Assuming that the USA is the trend-setter in the area of legal liability, we can expect those developments to eventually 'trickle down', to some extent, to other common law jurisdictions.

The stakes (and legal costs) in any kind of IP litigation can be quite high. For example, the long-running patent dispute that threatened to shut-down the entire Blackberry network finally settled for US$612 million. Legal costs in patent infringement suits are typically measured in the millions – which makes commercial settlements (regardless of the merits of a particular claim) a sometimes unavoidable consideration.

Key Issues

Key issues to be on the alert for when seeking an IP indemnity from a Manufacturer/Seller are:

1. That it extends to cover *allegations* of IP infringements – after all, you would not be faced with the allegation were it not for the fact that you were using the product;

2. That it is not expressed to operate on a verdict that is "finally awarded" by a court – this would mean that an initial court verdict would not be sufficient to trigger the obligation to indemnity. The affected party would be obliged to exhaust every legal appeal avenue to the highest court, before the contractual obligation to indemnify would even be triggered;

3. That the word "reasonable" does not appear in the indemnity wording. Limiting the amount of recovery to "reasonable" claims or covering "reasonable legal costs" would not be acceptable in an indemnity, as it would severely limit the amount or possibility of any recovery;

4. That there is no cap or ceiling on the amount of recovery permissible under such indemnity;

5. Ideally, it should extend to include protection against "all costs incurred by or awarded against" the party having the benefit of the indemnity;

6. Exercising care on any indemnity which attempts to restrict the operation of the indemnity to an IP breach or claim occurring in a particular geographical territory or location.

Force majeure

A *force majeure* event is an agreed event beyond the control of a party, which frustrates or postpones the ability of that party to perform its obligations under the contract. The key feature of a force majeure situation is that a force majeure event can be a temporary condition delaying performance. Much will, of course, will depend on the specific drafting of the force majeure clause.

The clause is intended to relieve that party from complying with its obligations under the contract for a certain period (usually, but not always, for the duration of the *force majeure* event).

In most jurisdictions, there is no law defining what actually constitutes a *force majeure* event. Hence, the definition will ultimately depend upon what the parties can agree upon and the way that such agreement is translated into the drafting of the force majeure clause.

Definitions will often include things such as "explosion, lightning, quarantine, epidemic, radiation, war, riot, terrorism, insurrection, Act of Parliament, or act of God".

It is generally to the benefit of any party supplying goods or services under a contract to have such a clause in their contract.

Golden Rule

A prudent Seller should always consider having a properly drafted *force majeure* clause in any contract, as a safeguard.

Key Issues

- The object of the clause is to create a set of *defined events*, where a party to the contract is <u>excused from performing its obligations</u>, due to such events (and for the duration of those events);

- Ensure that the list of events is as broad as you need it to be, eg industrial action;

- Avoid a force majeure clause that excludes any <u>*foreseeable*</u> event from the operation of the clause – after the events of 9/11, one can argue that almost anything is now foreseeable. For example, one could argue that tornadoes in the US Midwest are foreseeable, or cyclones/typhoons in tropical regions of the globe – the issue is, even if they are foreseeable, what can anyone do about them? That is to say, whilst they are occurring, commercial interruptions that are not within anyone's control are inevitable;

- An obligation to make a payment should not, generally, be subject to force majeure;

- Be wary of a clause that requires the party seeking the benefit of a force majeure clause (typically a Seller) having to make *"every"* effort to remedy a force majeure event. For a Seller, this could require the Seller being compelled into a situation of having to spend enormous amounts of money to overcome a force majeure event (eg having to airfreight heavy and expensive equipment at its own cost instead of sea freighting them. More appropriate might be the obligation to make *"reasonable efforts"* to overcome the effects of a force majeure event;

- In the list of the actual events which constitute a force majeure event, using the words *"including but not limited to…"* to describe them, will provide greater protection to the party seeking to benefit from this clause;

- It may be appropriate in some instances to limit the force majeure clause duration to an agreed period – such as 30, 60, 90 days or more. In that way, even if the force majeure event continues beyond that period, the parties are free to terminate the agreement and move on. This last issue would be of greater concern to a Buyer, in such an instance, who might wish to be free to move on.

Termination for convenience

The *termination for convenience* clause grants an extremely broad right for a Buyer to, unilaterally and without cause, terminate an existing (and often long-term) contract, without becoming liable for breach-of-contract damages.

Such clauses are drawn to limit the ability of the party being terminated to recover only *actual costs incurred* plus *profit on work <u>completed</u>*. Such clauses are generally drawn to preclude the recovery of antici-patory profit.

Termination for convenience clauses are not "normal" commercial terms. They are usually found in almost every government contract, however, corporations in the private sector are increasingly tending to mimic the trend for their use.

In general, such clauses operate unilaterally (only one party can terminate the contract for convenience) and therefore do not give the other party the certainty of tenure that a "normal" contract does.

Key Issues

If you absolutely must accept a termination for convenience clause, you should seek to negotiate more favourable terms on, at least, the following matters:

1. Reject the Clause (if you can);

2. include provision for reimbursement of the actual costs incurred in mobilising and demobilising in respect of any equipment and materials;

3. include provision for reimbursement of the costs of settling and paying termination settlements for *staff* dedicated to the contract;

4. include provision for reimbursement of the costs of settling and paying termination settlements for *subcontractors* dedicated to the contract;

5. lengthen the term of notice from the ubiquitous 30 days to, say, 90 or 180 days, or an even longer period, depending upon the relevant circumstances;

6. Make the clause operate reciprocally – so that either party can terminate for convenience;

7. Compulsory repurchase (at its original landed invoice cost) of any inventory held for this contract;

8. Negotiate a separate additional "termination" or "break" fee.

III

Time of the essence

This clause is used to make the concept of time an essential term of the contract. It often looks something like this:

> *Time is of the essence in* [**Party A** performing a certain action]

OR

> ***Party A*** *shall* [perform a certain action] *time being of the essence.*

Firstly, it is important to understand the meaning of the expression *essential term*. An essential term is a term *fundamental to the basis of the contract itself*; such that if it is not performed, alters the very nature of the contract itself.

In many jurisdictions, an essential term, once breached, gives rise to termination of the contract by the non-defaulting party. The non-defaulting party would then be entitled to sue the defaulting party for any loss suffered in respect of such termination including the concept of loss-of-bargain damages.

Golden Nugget

Take your time!

Often, it isn't the termination itself that causes the problems, it is the use of a well-placed *threat* of such termination occurring.

Consider where you and your customer ("Buyer") are locked into a long-term agreement which is proving to be enormously profitable to you. On a single occasion, you breach a time of the essence obligation.

When your customer comes to you saying:

"Our Board has asked that you show cause, why we should not terminate this agreement"

You instantly realise that such an expression is code for:

"what are you going to do for us (and give us), to stop us from wanting to terminate"?

Assuming the Buyer never had any intention to terminate, it has certainly has you positioned where they want you (in a position of vulnerability and fear). That vulnerability and fear is what will most likely drive you to offer price cuts and free goods/ services to sweeten the Buyer, in an effort to retain the Contract that you are in fear of losing.

Perhaps the contract was never really under threat, but by breaching a time of the essence obligation, you gave the Buyer a "free-kick" – and

> the savvy Buyer seized on the opportunity to score significant and valuable concessions, that you would never otherwise have made (or been required to make).

The idea of using a *time of the essence* clause, is to make the concept of time (as in the performance of a particular obligation in a contract) an essential term of the contract.

When using time of the essence, *the concept of reasonableness is excluded*. The breach of a time limit by as little as one minute could trigger a breach.

Indeed, the danger of making essential terms of all time stipulations in a contract, is obvious. Every action, under a contract, which is subject to a time limit, becomes an essential term. If such term is breached, it could then give rise to termination of the contract and an action for damages. In any given commercial contract, that could amount to thousands of individual potential instances of risk.

In some jurisdictions, the effect of the time of the essence concept has been called into question and there is no clear determination. However, prudence dictates that you assume the worst and thereby, avoid trouble. Your lawyer can best advise you of the specifics of your jurisdiction and your contractual situation.

Key issues

Time of the essence - Potential consequences in the event of breach:

1. Termination of contract

2. Loss of bargain damages

3. In practice, it could force you to incur additional costs to avoid breach (eg having to airfreight goods instead of by sea – at your own cost)

How do you negotiate such a clause?

- 1st prize is to *delete*

- 2nd prize is to *limit* its scope and application.

- If neither is successful, you could ask for it to operate *reciprocally*.

Golden Nugget

1. If a time of the essence obligation is to remain in a contract, in any form, are you being rewarded adequately for it?

2. A time of the essence obligation is a premium service – for example, if you want your letter delivered fast, it is like paying *pounds* to FEDEX, as against paying *pence* to the post office.

3. Any service that guarantees time or expedition – demands a higher charge for that service.

4. What are you getting in return?

▓▓▓

Assignment

An *assignment clause* is quite simply a transfer of rights, benefits and obligations under a contract from one party (called the *assignor*) to another party (called the *assignee*).

Parties often go to great lengths to select other parties prior to entering into a contract relationship with them. They apply a number of criteria judged to be important to ultimately select the other party they believe best fulfils such criteria. After such a rigorous process, a party will usually wish to ensure that it continues to deal with the entity it had selected.

Many will usually require the option of terminating the contract in the event of any attempt at substituting the other party or in the event of a *change of control* in the other party's company (see also **Change of control clause**). At the very least, many would find it desirable to have a process to have the final right of approval of any change in the other party.

Parties, therefore, tend to agree on the benefits of having an assignment clause in their contract, containing specified conditions restricting and governing the assignment of the one party's interest in the contract to another party. The assignment clause will usually contain a restriction preventing any assignment of such interest without the other's written consent. The primary reason being that another party proposing to take the place of the assignor will often be unknown to the other party.

In many contractual relationships, one of the parties tends to have the "upper hand" over the other. For example, in a tendering situation, the Buyer will usually have the upper hand over the Seller. In these situations, assignment clauses can often operate unilaterally preventing the tenderer from assigning whilst expressly permitting the Buyer to assign its interest at will and without the necessity of requiring the other party's approval.

In such a situation where an assignment clause permits a Seller to assign its interest, it will be common for there to be certain conditions allowing a Buyer to withhold consent to the assignment until:

---

1. **certain conditions prescribed by the assignment clause are satisfied by the Seller;**

   For example, the Buyer may wish to withhold consent until the existing breaches of the agreement by the Seller have been remedied.

---

2. **the steps prescribed by the assignment clause have been followed by the Seller (and the incoming party) and;**

   For example, the Seller may have to follow certain steps regarding the form and timing of notice to the Buyer of the proposed assignment. Also regarding the timely provision of relevant information requested by the Buyer.

3. **certain criteria prescribed by the assignment clause have been met by the incoming party.**

   For example, the new Seller may have to establish proof of their reputation, financial strength and stability, a particular type of insurance coverage, trade or bank references, and demonstrated skills to be able to perform certain specialised tasks etc. These criteria must be satisfied by the new Seller to a standard that is no less favourable to the Buyer.

Change of control clause

A useful supplement to an assignment clause is the *change of control* clause. From a Buyer's perspective, this will govern the situation where there is a change in the ownership or control of the Seller.

For example, a Seller might be acquired by a company, which the Buyer does not consider suitable or with which the Buyer specifically wishes to avoid having any dealings. Another reason might be that the acquiring entity did not have the financial strength and stability required by the Buyer.

A Buyer wishing to broaden the scope of the change of control provision, would generally also extend it to capture any change of control over the Seller's *parent company*.

A further way of broadening the change of control clause is to define one of the events constituting a change of control to be any change in the *effective* control of the company. This caters for situations where an event does not constitute a change in the *legal or ownership* control of the company, but in reality does create a change of *actual* control.

Examples of such an event could be:

- the appointment or removal of all (or the majority) of the directors or other equivalent officers of the Seller; or

- giving directions with respect to the operating and financial policies of the Seller, with which the directors or other equivalent officers of the Seller are obliged to comply.

A change of control clause will generally define the events constituting a change of control. It will generally provide that any change of control (that falls within such definition) will:

- trigger a certain set of events such as termination; or

- may be *deemed* to be an assignment. Such a deeming provision will then trigger the same information and approval processes necessary in an assignment situation.

Future changes to the law

There are obviously competing interests on the issue of changes to the law.

Some contracts will contain provisions dealing with future change in the law or other administrative regulations, which could affect the parties, services or price.

For example, the introduction of a new tax on the goods or services being provided by the Seller immediately triggers the question: *who will bear this new cost?* Remember that it will be a cost or other impediment not previously contemplated by the parties when the contract was negotiated and entered into. What happens if the existing rate of Value Added Tax rises? If there is a decrease (an unprecedented move which occurred in late 2008 during the global financial crisis), is a Seller obliged to share the saving generated.

A prudent Seller will wish to include a clause dealing with the issue to avoid any doubt that the

Buyer will bear the risk of changes to the law.

With an appropriately drafted clause, the introduction of a new tax would enable the Seller to pass on the effect of the new tax to the Buyer, thereby preserving the Seller's margins and profitability.

Governing law and jurisdiction

Parties need to agree upon the applicable law governing the contract document, in the event of any dispute or call for interpretation of the contents of the document.

The contract should specify under which particular Country/State's law the contract will be governed and interpreted. For example, such a statement will specifically declare the contract to be governed by and interpreted under the laws of New South Wales, the laws of England, the State of California, USA, etc.

This is usually accompanied by a statement of the jurisdiction or *forum* (place) for the settlement of any disputes arising.

Usually, the party drafting the agreement chooses its own local jurisdiction, in the absence of any other arrangement.

Key Issues

1. Where possible, ensure that the applicable law and jurisdiction are one and the same – It can have a dramatic impact on the <u>economics</u> of any dispute, as it is an expensive proposition to run a court case in another country from your own, especially so when it is based on the laws and rules of a third country.

2. If it is a jurisdiction other than your own, factor the additional potential costs into your overall risk assessment of the contract.

3. Understand whether the selection of "exclusive" or "non-exclusive" jurisdiction is the more appropriate for your situation

4. This can have a drastic effect on the <u>interpretation and meaning</u> of contract clauses

5. Enormously influences the ability to make a "<u>commercial decision</u>" on a liability issue. *Is there any exposure in the USA?*

6. Determine whether, the laws of the country of execution of the agreement, *automatically determines* the selection of applicable law and/or jurisdiction.

For a more detailed examination of jurisdiction clauses and an explanation of the differences between exclusive and non-exclusive jurisdiction, you should consult *The Managers Guide to Understanding Commonly Used Contract Terms: Boilerplate Clauses*, the fourth volume in the *Commercial Contracts for Managers Series*.

Retention of title (ROT) or Romalpa clause

A Retention of Title clause – is sometimes called a Romalpa clause, named after the landmark ROT case, where these issues were first explored in depth – one of the parties in that case was a company called *Romalpa Aluminium Ltd*. The name has since been "adopted" by lawyers as a short-form way of saying "retention of title clause".

The concept behind the clause can be expressed as simply as follows:

Risk of loss and damage to the goods shall pass to the Buyer upon delivery. Title shall only pass to the Buyer upon payment in full.

Many common law jurisdictions require a more comprehensive version of the clause.

Under a ROT clause, the Buyer of goods takes possession of the goods but does not acquire legal title to them unless and until the goods are paid for in full.

The clause is designed to protect the Seller, as it provides for the repossession of the goods, by the Seller, from the Buyer who fails to pay or goes into liquidation.

The right of repossession is a very powerful right. However, what happens if the goods are no longer available on the Buyer's premises to repossess? Note that in many business situations, a Buyer of goods will typically resell those goods. For example, a retailer of computer equipment might purchase computer systems and peripherals for resale to government or business, or even to members of the public.

To further complicate matters, consider a situation where that same retailer purchases individual components from various suppliers and creates its own brand of computer system, for resale. Note that it is not actually reselling the individual components in the same manner in which they were purchased. In this case, those goods are being incorporated into another product for resale.

Think of a builder purchasing concrete, steel and glass and incorporating those into a building.

What happens in the event of such a resale? A ROT clause usually provides that if Buyer resells the goods, it must account to the original Seller for the proceeds outstanding.

A properly drafted ROT clause should impose obligations upon the Buyer to physically segregate and specially mark stock that is subject to ROT. Futhermore, in the event of any resale, that the proceeds must be kept in a separate and specific account. In effect, the Buyer is being obliged to quarantine either stock or the proceeds from the sale of that stock.

Golden Rule

A ROT clause must be in the original contract between Seller and Buyer.

To simply add it is as an afterthought, on a delivery invoice, is usually not sufficient.

It is particularly interesting to note that in some jurisdictions such as Australia, courts have held that a properly drafted ROT clause actually creates a trust in favour of the original owner of the resulting proceeds of sale. In the event that the Buyer company goes into liquidation, such a trust is usually sufficient to defeat a claim brought by the liquidator on behalf of any unsecured creditors.

As an accounting note, any inventory or stock held by the Buyer company - which is the subject of a ROT provision - should not be shown on the Buyer company's balance sheet as "stock on hand", since it is not actually "owned".

Legal ownership is reserved to the original owner, pending receipt of full payment.

In other jurisdictions, the concept of ROT is incorporated into a larger legislative framework – for example, in New Zealand, there is legislation called the Personal Property Securities Act (PPSA).

Under the PPSA, the following is required to ensure that ROT is valid and enforceable:

- Customer is required to acknowledge that the ROT is a security interest;

- Customer must agree to grant you a security interest

- Customer must sign a copy of the terms and conditions to evidence such agreement (note that their conduct alone, in accepting these terms, is not enough)

- Seller must then proceed to register that security interest – this can be done online 24/7 and attracts a nominal fee.

Note that, under the PPSA, the retention of title arrangement will <u>not be enforceable</u> unless all of these steps are followed.

"All contingencies allowed for" clause

This clause typically provides that the Seller has allowed for any possible contingency or problem that could arise has been taken into account and is included in the price quoted by the Seller. It is used to try and protect a Buyer from variations costs that could be charged to it by a Seller in the event of some (usually unexpected or unforeseen) contingency.

The nature of the fact that some such contingencies are going to be unexpected or unforeseen by either party, makes this type of clause an extremely risky proposition for a Seller. In effect, a Seller is being asked to guarantee that nothing will go wrong, and that if it does, that the Seller will take care of it at its own cost.

The transfer of risk onto the Seller is a massive one, to say the least. A prudent Seller, when confronted with such a clause (or any clause that transfers risk to the Seller), must ask itself: "What's in it for me?"

The "All contingencies allowed for" clause can look something like this:

> *Seller represents and warrants that it fully comprehends the requirements and contingencies for providing Services and it shall examine the Work Site for any additional or special requirements and contingencies prior to performing Services.*

The effect of accepting it...

- It shifts the onus of finding errors contingencies or discrepancies onto the Seller.

- In essence, these clauses are used to try and penalize the Seller in the event that they fail to carry out sufficient enquiry and investigation to uncover an error.

- This form of obligation is becoming more commonly used in the mining industry.

- The "all contingencies considered" clause is a transfer of risk onto the Seller

Yet another way of accept a huge transfer of risk is acceptance of the following type of clause:

> *Seller represents and warrants that it shall not perform any aspect of the Services that it knows <u>or should know</u> cannot be performed in conformity with the provisions of this Agreement. If Seller determines that it cannot perform Services in conformity with those provisions, Seller shall immediately advise Buyer and work with Buyer to develop a mutually satisfactory resolution. Seller further represents and warrants that <u>it shall ascertain whether any drawings and specifications applicable to the Services are at</u>*

> *variance with Law or with good engineering and*
> *operational practices before beginning any Services.*
> *Seller shall immediately notify Buyer in writing of*
> *any such variance and ensure that the necessary*
> *changes are made before proceeding with the part of*
> *the Services affected*

The nett effects of such an outrageously blatant clause are:

- It shifts the burden to the Seller according to what it <u>should know</u>, rather than focusing on what was <u>actually</u> known or discovered.

- The clause also obliges the Seller to ascertain whether any of the drawings or specs are at variance with *"good engineering and operational practices <u>before beginning</u> any Services"*.

- In other words, Seller is required to give its blessing to the specifications developed and provided by the Buyer. In the event that such specifications turn out to be incorrect or defective in some way, the problem becomes the Seller's, due to its breach of this warranty.

- Ordinarily, a defect in a Buyer's specification would be their problem – this clause attempts to switch the incidence of the risk and transfer it entirely into an unsuspecting Buyer's lap.

> ### *Golden Rule*
>
> Beware of any contract clause that deals with what you "*ought to have known*" or "*should*" have known.
>
> Such matters should only be based on what is <u>actually</u> known to you.

Beware of terms similar to the following:

<u>The Seller shall ensure</u>, and hereby warrants to the Buyer, <u>that all materials</u> and standards of workmanship:

1. *used in carrying out the work under the Contract; or*

2. *incorporated into the Goods,*

and whether:

1. *chosen by the Seller; or*

2. *the subject of a particular requirement of the Contract; or*

3. *which the Contract stipulates to be a preferred material, or material from a preferred sub-supplier,*

<u>are in accordance with the requirements of the Contract and</u> that the Goods shall comply with all of the requirements of the Contract and be of good quality and <u>fit for their intended purposes</u>

The effect of accepting it:

- This places the Seller in a potentially invidious position as regards specific contract requirements – it is required to warrant those materials selected by the Buyer.

- However, if it discovers that the materials so specified are not suitable, it risks being in breach of contract if the Buyer rejects its recommendations.

- If this clause is to be accepted, there should be a mechanism where the Seller is no longer responsible where it has made a recommendation to the Buyer and that the Buyer rejects such recommendation

Golden Nugget

Compliance with Head-Contract terms you have never seen.

- Often, a subcontractor may be asked to sign an acknowledgment of receipt of the Head Contract (the contract between the Buyer of your services and its Principal), when in fact, none was ever supplied.

- There is an enormous risk in accepting liability for terms that you, as a subcontractor have never seen or reviewed.

- You cannot accept these without placing yourself at grave risk, particularly if that head Contract contains onerous indemnities, consequential loss provisions and no limits to liability – and you won't know what the Head Contract contains until you see it.

III

Limitation of liability clauses

The clause allows a party to the contract to introduce an upper limit of its liability either in defined circumstances, or indeed, in a complete and blanket manner.

Where possible, it is a prudent method of managing and limiting one's risk. Companies will often strive to limit their liability to an amount equivalent to the contract sum or less (or sometimes even to limiting their liability to specific repair or replacement cost of a particular product).

Whether it is possible to do so, and if so its effectiveness, will vary depending on the jurisdiction of the contract.

Golden Nugget

Understand that when another party to a contract attempts to limit its liability to you, it is effectively transferring that risk to you.

Your acceptance of their attempts to limit their liability, effectively constitute your acceptance of that transfer of risk to you.

Consider the relationship of such attempts by the other party to limit its liability to you, with the terms of your own liability insurance coverage – they need to be in alignment.

Note that in most countries, there is specific consumer legislation (that prohibits any attempt to exclude the operation of its provisions), which either curtails or prohibits any attempt to limit liability of sales of certain consumer goods to end-user consumers.

However, in a business-to-business context, there are usually no similar legislative restrictions pertaining to the use of limitation of liability clauses.

Beware of attempts to limit liability to you, where you are the "middleman" in a transaction. Consider the following example:

Case Study: An electrical distributor with a "come what may" attitude to limitation of liability clauses

Shortcut City is a Seller of consumer electrical appliances. It sources its most popular range of appliances from an Asian manufacturer called **Kumquat Mai**. It has an agreement with that manufacturer - we will refer to that agreement the "upstream contract".

Shortcut City sells the products it imports from its chain of stores.

Sales are to consumers (there is no actual written agreement with its customer), but **Shortcut City** is bound by local consumer protection laws – so it cannot limit its liability downstream to the consumer.

However, in the distribution agreement between **Kumquat Mai** and **Shortcut City** there are strict provisions whereby **Kumquat Mai** limits its liability to **Shortcut City** to the sum of US$50,000. The limitation of liability clause, in part, read something like this:

The Supplier's total aggregate liability to the Buyer or any Third Parties in contract or in tort (including, without limitation, in negligence) for, or in respect of, any loss or damage suffered by the Buyer or Third Parties arising out of a breach or other act or omission in connection with this Distributor Agreement is limited to the sum of US$50,000 in the aggregate.

Shortcut City's CEO, **Myra Mains**, chose not to have the agreement reviewed by a lawyer, as she had signed many of these contracts before without a problem. Also, she knew that the store chain had a long relationship with **Kumquat Mai**, which she considered was an adequate guarantee of safety.

Kumquat Mai's quality control was certainly not up to world's best practice standards, but their pricing was attractive and gave the stores a healthy profit margin.

Due to the transfer of production to a new and cheaper facility, the failure rates of **Kumquat Mai's** products begin to skyrocket. Epidemic failures abounded.

Product failures in some of the electrical components began to cause house fires and the electrocution of several customers. Consumer lawsuits against **Shortcut City** began to increase and multiply.

The nation's Consumer Regulator finally ordered that all **Kumquat Mai** products be recalled from the market. **Shortcut City** was compelled to carry out the recall itself and make good on all consumer claims – all this at a cost of several million pounds.

In seeking contribution from the manufacturer, **Shortcut City** was able to produce comprehensive documentary evidence:

1. that the products' failure rates had skyrocketed;

2. of the legitimacy of the claims received from consumers

3. of the cost of mounting a product recall

Kumquat Mai did not disagree with any of this. Their response was simply to rely on the limitation of liability clause contained in their agreement.

The end result was that **Kumquat Mai** remitted to **Shortcut City** the equivalent of US$10,000, after deducting monies owed to it by **Shortcut City** for past product purchases (a large proportion of which were defective).

The conclusion to **Shortcut City's** story was rather more bleak:

1. It was millions of pounds out of pocket

2. It was engaged in a bitter legal wrangle with its insurer over reimbursement of claims made against it

3. Its distribution agreement with **Kumquat Mai** was terminated.

4. Shortly after which, the company's high flying CEO **Myra Mains** was publicly fired by the Board in humiliating (and career-ending) manner.

5. **Shortcut City's** reputation was in tatters and had lost the confidence of consumers, who deserted the stores.

6. The saga culminated in the appointment of liquidators, as the once market-leading chain of stores finally went under.

Had there not been a limitation of liability clause in the agreement with **Kumquat Mai**, the end to the story could well have been a different one for the store and for **Myra Mains**.

Imagine if the limitation of liability clause had contained something like the following amendments:

Except in respect of any liability which the Supplier may have in relation to personal injury or death, to the extent permitted by _law and despite any implication arising from_ _any other clause in the Distributor Agreement,_ the Supplier's total aggregate liability to the Buyer ~~or Third Parties~~ in contract or in tort ~~(including, without limitation, in negligence)~~ for, or in respect of, any loss or damage suffered by the Buyer or Third Parties arising out of a breach or other act or omission in connection with this Distributor Agreement is limited to the sum of US$50,000 in the aggregate. _Expressly excluded from this_ _limitation of liability is any liability of Supplier_ _for any Product warranty obligation, Epidemic_ _Defects, personal injury, death or property_ _damage caused by or arising from the use of_ _the Products by any person_.

Chapter 4

SOME COMMONLY USED LEGAL EXPRESSIONS

▌▌▌

"Reasonable"

In most Common Law Jurisdictions, the term is used to mean "appropriate, ordinary or usual in the circumstances", it can also mean "just" or "rational".

The term is often used in situations where a precise measurement is neither appropriate nor possible. For example, where a contract calls for a breach to be "remedied within a *reasonable* time."

It is also used to "soften" the impact of an obligation. For example, where:

"A shall pay B's legal costs".

Introducing the word "reasonable" can help to narrow down and "soften" this obligation, so that the assessment of costs cannot be infinite or indefinite. To restate the above obligation would then read:

> *"A is obliged to pay B's reasonable legal costs".*

This has the effect of restricting the extent of the obligation to pay costs to something that is "reasonable".

There are pros and cons to using imprecise terms such "reasonable" or "substantial" or "material". Whether they are advantages or disadvantages depends upon your perspective – whether it is in your interests to create a little ambiguity or, whether that would work against you.

Issues

Such terms are not precise, definite or accurately measurable.

They provide the party against whom the obligation is being enforced, an opportunity to introduce uncertainty and argue about what is, or is not, "reasonable" or "substantial" or "material".

Remember using the term "reasonable", can soften the impact of an obligation. Where you are a party seeking to enforce the terms of a contract (where there has been a breach), the word "reasonable" makes enforcement less certain and a little more problematic – what can often occur is that the parties become embroiled in arguments about what constitutes "reasonable" behaviour or conduct.

Depending on your point of view, this can either be useful or detrimental.

Golden Nugget

Being reasonable

Beware of connecting the concept of "reasonable" being applied to or included in any kind of indemnity.

For example, altering an indemnity in respect of legal fees to "reasonable" legal fees, means that the indemnity is not really an indemnity - the issue is where every dollar of legal fees incurred becomes subject to question and is required to pass thru the filter of what is "reasonable".

An indemnity, in the strict sense, is necessarily a blank cheque, that in this case, would cover <u>all</u> legal expenses.

Obviously an indemnitee (in whose favour an indemnity operates) has a real problem if the indemnitor (party giving the indemnity) is able to scrutinise the legal costs, with the benefit of hindsight and effectively question everything retrospectively - even down to law-firm hourly rates, as there is always going to be a cheaper firm available.

▌▌▌

"Forthwith"

This term was traditionally used with much more frequency than it is today. With the current trend towards "plain English" drafting, and in a quest for greater certainty, the term is somewhat out of vogue.

In most Common Law jurisdictions, the term often means "promptly" or "without delay".

However, in some situations, it could also be argued to mean "within a reasonable time having regard to the circumstances".

Obviously, if the person drafting the Contract has a desire for the term to mean "promptly and without delay", the use of the word "forthwith" is probably not the best choice, given the potential uncertainty.

A better choice would be using words such as:

"immediately"

OR

"within "X days from ....".

"Such consent not to be unreasonably withheld".

Some contracts contemplate the necessity of having to obtain consent from the other party to the contract, to do a particular act or thing. For example, permission for one party to assign their interest in a contract to a third party, will usually require the consent of the other party to the agreement.

The issue with obtaining such consent occurs where one wishes to remove a discretion to withhold that consent for any reason (regardless of whether that reason is a valid one or otherwise).

In such instances, the phrase: "such consent not to be unreasonably withheld" immediately follows within the provision stipulating the necessity for the obtaining of that consent.

Whilst the use of the phrase helps to plug a loophole, on its own, it fails to cover the *length of time* within which such consent must be granted.

Accordingly, a party not intending to grant such consent, might be able to find a way around doing so, by insisting that it is not actually *withholding* the consent but merely *delaying* it. Putting aside any equitable considerations, where such delay is not contemplated by the clause, there is no guidance or relief to be found under the terms of the contract, for dealing with such a situation.

For these reasons, the more prudent drafting would be:

"such consent not to be unreasonably withheld <u>or delayed</u>".

"For the avoidance of doubt"

This phrase appears to be in more common use in Britain and Australia and has gradually crept into American legal drafting.

The phrase is often used to give an example that is not necessarily exhaustive.

Some argue that the term can be deleted from drafting as the language following it does not alter in any meaningful way. The rationale being that it is usually stating the blinding obvious and that the clarification can be provided without the use of those words. For example:

> *"These terms may be executed in any number of counterparts and all counterparts taken together will constitute one document. For the avoidance of doubt, a facsimile transmission of a signed counterpart shall be acceptable".*

Proponents against "for the avoidance of doubt" suggest that the above term could be drafted as follows:

> *"These terms may be signed in any number of counterparts and all counterparts taken together will constitute one document including a facsimile transmission of a signed counterpart".*

The deletion of the words "for the avoidance of doubt" above may well alter the meaning of the clause, particularly when one bears in mind the maxim *"expressio unius est exclusio alterios"* (the expression of one thing is the exclusion of another). Whilst the maxim is not a rule of law, it is an aid to construction.

The term "for the avoidance of doubt" is often used when providing an illustrative example of the application of a clause.

Some consider that the words *"it being understood"* or *"thus"* can also serve the same function as the use of *"for the avoidance of doubt"*, by attempting to clarify preceding language.

One other expression also used, to assist in clarifying the intention of the person drafting the document, is: "to the intent that...". Following on from the above example, such a clause might read:

"These terms may be signed in any number of counterparts and all counterparts taken together will constitute one document, to the intent that a facsimile transmission of a signed counterpart shall be permissible for the purposes of this clause".

"Shall"

Advocates of modern contract drafting are opposed to the use of the word "shall" in expressing a legal obligation.

Those advocates suggest the word "shall" being replaced with the more strident-sounding "must", or, even using the word "will", in reference to the performance of an obligation.

The use of the word "must" in expressing an obligation can tend to seem "pushy" or "in your face". Although some might argue that lawyers may be unconcerned at the prospect of being perceived as "pushy".

The use of the word "will" in expressing an obligation has a tendency to be problematic. In everyday usage, the word "will" conveys the meaning of "at some future time". This can cause difficulties if an obligation requires immediate action. The use of the word "will" may have the tendency to actually soften such immediacy.

The more traditional Contract drafters tend to prefer the use of the "shall" as a "tried and true" formula but also for the reason that the use of "shall' carries with it the implication of "duty".

Some will assert that lawyers tend to overuse "shall". For example, in a definitions section of a contract, the use of the word "shall", could probably be avoided:

"Day" shall mean business day...

In contrast to:

"Day" means business day...

Or, take this example:

"This Agreement shall be governed by the Laws of England"

Could probably be more succinctly expressed as:

"This Agreement is governed by the Laws of England".

▓▓▓

"Including but not limited to".

Before we look at the meaning of the term itself, it is important to know the Latin maxim behind it *"expressio unius est exclusio alterius"*, which means the expression of one is the exclusion of the other.

Where a general statement is made in a contract clause and a list of examples follows it, then that list of examples can then be treated as an <u>exhaustive</u> list.

This means, if it is not on the list, it may be ignored.

This is a danger whenever a contract clause lists specific events. For example, in a *force majeure* clause, there may be a list of defined events that constitute a force majeure event:

- *Storm*
- *Tempest*
- *Typhoon*
- *Act of God*
- *Act of terrorism*
- *Outbreak of war*
- *Civil unrest*

- *Riot*

- *Civil commotion.*

In the above example, without any additional qualification, the risk is that the above list of defined events is the <u>only</u> list, and that if an event occurs that does not appear on the list, then it will not trigger the operation of the force majeure clause.

The use of the words *"including but not limited to"* preceding the above list, would have the effect of including the specified events, but the list itself would not be limited to be an exhaustive list. Accordingly, other events not listed, could still be sufficient to trigger the operation of the force majeure clause.

Another useful rule to be aware of is the *ejusdem generis* rule. This operates where a Contract clause contains a series of specific words, followed by more general words – in that respect it differs from the *"expressio unius"* rule.

For example:

"assets" means motor vehicles, machinery, tools and any other thing owned by the business

Does the above definition include a computer and its software? This may be open to question, because the general words could be read-down to infer that the clause refers only to things in the machinery and tools category.

Some Common Law Courts in recent times have confirmed that the *expressio unius* and *ejusdem generis* rules are not <u>automatically</u> applied.

However, prudent and conservative drafters will tend to tailor their drafting to not fall foul of the application of either of these two rules of construction.

▌▌▌

"mutatis mutandis"

Is a Latin expression meaning "with the necessary changes being made".

For example, a confidentiality agreement might contain the following provision:

If you disclose any Confidential Information to your officers, employees, agents or advisers, you must ensure that:

a)   the disclosure is on a "need to know basis" necessary solely for the Project; and

*b)   such third parties agree to observe the terms of this Agreement **mutatis mutandis** as if they were a party to it and execute written confidentiality undertakings in our favour to that effect.*

If one was to use the term in an everyday conversational situation, to illustrate the point, the following exchange could be envisioned:

> "*The reasons given by Boris apply **mutatis mutandis** to me*".

Part 2

THE MACRO
PERSPECTIVE

Chapter 5

CONTRACT MANAGEMENT

░░░

What is contract management?

Contract management, in the context used in this book, concerns the management of the large volume of contract documents encountered every year by many organisations. The problem is essentially this:

How can an organisation effectively manage and legally scrutinise each and every contract coming in through its door?

The problem is not necessarily confined to companies engaged in tendering but extends to any company that enters into contracts on a regular basis. Typically, there could be:

1. upstream contracts (purchases from suppliers); and

2. downstream contract (sales to customers).

The upstream/downstream division could apply to a manufacturer (sourcing components from various suppliers), a catering contractor, a cleaning contractor, a distributor of any kind, and so on. The permutations are virtually limitless.

Some of the primary issues covered in this section relate to the methods of contract management, compliance procedures and systems. These are potentially, the areas of the greatest risk of exposure to liability for many companies.

It is all very well to understand commercial contracts, however, if there is no method or system in place dealing with the way that contracts are managed, very few contracts will ever be subjected to review.

Consequently, very little of the knowledge acquired from the *Commercial Contracts for Managers Series*, will ever be applied.

Given the large number of contracts and tenders that most organisation deal with on a daily basis, it is important to ensure that sufficient controls and safeguards exist, to adequately manage the legal risk or exposure underlying each of the contracts entered into by the organisation.

Businesses typically deal with a large number of contracts each year. The problem arises from a combination of both the size and complexity of those contracts and (more often than not) the extremely tight deadlines faced.

The problem tends to manifest itself in situations where a company is frequently engaged in tendering processes to win work.

Generally, two major steps need to be taken to confront this problem. Organisations should, where possible:

1) devise and produce a contract management policy; and

2) standardise the forms of contract for each business unit throughout the organisation.

Effective contract management

Effective contract management can:

- Empower selected staff to apply their initiative and experience.

- Establish parameters within which selected staff can confidently and comfortably operate, knowing that they are doing all they can to safeguard the interests of the organisation.

- Have everyone doing what they do best (ie to help run the business) without getting bogged down in wads of contract documentation.

- Present a professional and polished image to customers in contract negotiations.

In many businesses, adequate controls need to be considered. In devising such controls and procedures, they must be of a sufficient standard to be:

- practically workable and adding real value to business processes;

- easy to follow;

- clear and unequivocal; and

- enforced to ensure universal adoption throughout the business.

It is important to ensure that any improvements instituted be organically able to cope with future acquisitions and proposed growth.

It is of questionable benefit to put into place an ad-hoc contract management infrastructure that will be rendered obsolete as soon as there is another acquisition or phase of growth. A system that needs to be constantly reinvented every year or two creates more problems than it solves.

Consequences of ineffective contract management

Because of the lack of time available, and the scarcity of human resources, contracts may sometimes be entered into that do not fully protect the interests of a tenderer.

As a result, companies selling their goods and/or services, may find themselves bound to unreasonably harsh terms in a contract, ultimately eroding their forecasted profitability. In some instances, harsh contract terms can even cause large losses on a contract. For example, giving blanket indemnities beyond what should reasonably be covered, such as the instance where a Seller indemnifies the Buyer for the Buyer's own negligence.

Another instance might be where a Seller finds itself in a situation where its prices are fixed for an inordinately long period of time. Where its initial estimates proved to be incorrect or optimistic, the Seller winds up in a loss-making situation, from which there is no escape.

Two issues in contract management

From a legal and risk standpoint, contract management is one of the most critical issues facing an organisation. There is a need for the formulation of adequate policies and procedures, together with the provision of a proper and workable infrastructure capable of growing as the organisation grows.

The two primary issues that must be dealt with are:

1. the selection of the appropriate method to be utilised to assess and evaluate client tenders and incoming contract documents; and

2. For situations where the organisation uses or is asked to provide a contract document, having a standard suite of contract documents is required that:

   a) are updated and disseminated centrally from one source, to ensure that all relevant persons have an up-to-date copy of the latest version; and

   b) its sales force understands (through training) and is able to discuss and elaborate key contract terms with clients in a professional manner.

The inherent conflict of interest

There is an inherent conflict of interest in the way that many organisations scrutinise and evaluate incoming contracts (that is, contracts submitted to the organisation by another party). They may either:

- allow the *operations* part of the business to carry out such a task. The rationale being that they are the persons that will end up actually providing the goods and/or services that are the subject of the contract. Therefore, they will be best placed to know whether they will be able to work to the contract; or

- entrust the process of incoming contract evaluation to their *business development* staff (sales persons). The rationale for this is that they are the "prospectors" for the organisation and have a broad knowledge of the organisation's systems and capabilities.

Certainly, the input of both sales and operations people is always useful and valuable in relation to assessing the viability of commercial aspects of a deal. There is always a place for their input and viewpoint to provide a practical and "real-world" perspective to any contract review.

Their value, however, will not usually extend to providing a proper assessment of the *legal* aspects and risks of a particular transaction.

The primary reason is that salespeople are driven by other priorities and motivations. The zeal to close a deal may, in some instances, compromise the judgment of that salesperson into accepting unduly onerous terms. Often, the rewards of salespersons are based on the number of deals and/or the volume of business brought into the organisation. The organisation's compliance with the terms of contract then becomes someone else's problem. Therefore, allowing commission-based salespeople to be the sole evaluators of incoming contracts, could be said by some, to be akin to allowing the proverbial fox to guard the chickens.

Sometimes, operations personnel may (with the best of intentions) be tempted to think that they can overcome a badly-worded contract document, by good management and impeccable customer-service. Unfortunately, the reality is that relationships cannot always overcome bad contract terms.

The only way to maintain control over the outcome of the contract review process is to have a policy in place at the *front end* of the process and to enforce it.

Case study
How differing incentive structures affect contract evaluations
Operations

Problem: The "monthly numbers" mindset. This is the environment in which most line managers are judged and held accountable. This produces little interest in making longer-term investment decisions.

Example: Where an organisation has a high worker injury problem with a high number of claims and escalating premiums. Seeking solutions by expenditure on Occupational Health and Safety prevention and training does not produce a bottom-line return in the following month to the manager making such an expenditure. Another example might be an operations manager who might make some significant concessions when negotiating an indemnity clause, since it might be perceived as not having any immediate bottom-line effect.

Solution: Budgeting needs be revised to make provisions for these kinds of longer-term investment strategies. Managers' incentive programmes should be designed with these types of decisions in mind.

Business development (sales)

Problem: In some organisations, the emphasis is on winning new business and boosting revenues, rather than on the quality and profitability of those contracts.

Example: From 10 contracts "won" by sales staff, only two turn out to be profitable, the unprofitable ones could be set-off against the profits earned in the two profitable ones. The difficulty here lies in attributing the responsibility for any such unprofitability (eg, whether it was due to a change in change in circumstances, incorrect estimating, or whether the operations side of the contract is being badly managed, etc).

Solution: Ideally, incentive structures could be geared towards a shift to winning profitable business. Incentives could be linked to global profitability of all contracts generated by the business development department.

Chapter 6

TO CENTRALISE OR DECENTRALISE CONTRACT EVALUATIONS?

▌▌▌

Remember that a contract management system is a part of an organisation's greater overall compliance system. Therefore, a general understanding of compliance becomes necessary at this point.

▌▌▌

Centralised Approach

This is where a designated person/department (usually a legal department, in a large corporation) reviews all contracts.

For most organisations, the centralised approach to contract evaluation is the preferred model to adopt. This is particularly so given the greater control this approach allows in relation to compliance issues. History often demonstrates that allowing (legally) unqualified persons to manage contractual risk leads to greater costs being incurred in losses, litigation and compromised corporate reputations.

Where a company has acquired other companies or businesses and is in the process of *integrating* the acquired businesses into its own, the centralised approach has a tendency to be the favoured approach.

The newly acquired businesses then learn that they are part of something bigger and are required to conform to their parent company's way of doing things. This can often prove to be painful, especially at the outset. It is a pain that can be overcome. The centralised approach helps to eliminate the "us" and "them" mindset that can be typical where newly-acquired companies or businesses are being integrated.

There are certainly other aspects of the business that are better managed by decentralising the functions. *Compliance is usually not one of those functions.*

The benefits to an organisation are the tighter controls it can exercise and the knowledge of what risks the business is taking on a day-to-day basis.

I have seen this proven in a number of larger organisations, particularly in the area of compliance, where centralising the process raised possible areas of non-compliance *before* prosecutions were issued against the organisation.

Arguments against a centralised approach

One of the primary disadvantages to having a centralised system is the potential for the legal department (or sole in-house lawyer) to become a "bottleneck". Especially in instances where a company mandates that every single agreement be passed through that legal department.

The simple fact is that, in such a situation, a sole lawyer or small legal department cannot cope with the amount of work generated by a typical organisation. A legal department is a *service* department and should therefore do everything possible to avoid becoming an organisational bottleneck.

As a consequence, the process becomes totally chaotic and prioritising becomes almost impossible. This is because there are often many time-sensitive issues in any organisation.

However, as many time management experts will attest, those tasks carrying the most urgency are not necessarily those of the highest level of importance or priority to the organisation as a whole.

Therefore, the level of importance of a task ultimately depends upon the persons with the "ownership" thereof; to the extent that persons who scream loudest tend to obtain priority. Such a situation is not of benefit to the organisation as a whole.

The legal department often ends up jammed with the workload with even simple contract reviews taking weeks and sometimes months. In frustration, some managers may even be tempted to either bypass the review process (with its attendant risks) or brief the matter to an external lawyer. In the latter process, the manager may bypass the internal lawyer's management procedures for external law firms.

Overly centralising the process also robs managers of the feeling of autonomy as their "baby" is placed into the hands of a (sometimes) distant legal department with little understanding of the nature of the transaction, its commercial context or its strategic importance to the organisation.

Also, due to time constraints, the in-house lawyer usually has little knowledge of the personalities of the parties concerned, who have often been in negotiations for a considerable period by the time the paperwork hits the lawyer's desk. These details can often be of significant importance in understanding the negotiating perspective of both parties.

Consequences of decentralising compliance functions

In a decentralised environment, the organisation's head office would, generally, not become aware of a problem until after some escalation of the issue. Naturally, by that stage, the problem can become much more significant. Additional time and other resources are then necessary to deal with, what previously was perhaps only a minor problem.

Of course, this has the potential to lead to consequences far beyond their original local or regional effects. In the event of adverse publicity, the organisation's existing customers may raise queries. Furthermore, potential customers may form a view of the organisation based on such media reports.

Sometimes, a manager will attempt to fix a problem to avoid having to bring the problem to the notice of its head office. Such actions are invariably detrimental to the entire company, which is deprived of the opportunity and benefit of early intervention.

In such events, prosecuting authorities are quick to notice the lack of head office controls and supervision over regional offices. This lack of knowledge and control makes it much more difficult to conduct a defence or to convince the prosecuting authorities that the organisation takes such responsibilities seriously.

This becomes especially relevant in the areas such as occupational health and safety legislation, which in some jurisdictions, carries *personal* liability for the directors of the company. The sanctions extend to include not only fines, but also terms of imprisonment, in the most extreme cases. Such incidents often receive media attention as well as the close scrutiny of a number of government authorities, some of which you may not even had heard of previously.

Most organisations centralise their most fundamental processes:

- finance;
- human resources; and
- procurement processes.

They are functions of critical importance to the business. For most organisations, the areas of legal and compliance should be no different.

###

Integration of business units

Another potential source of conflict can arise in an organisation that is an assembled collection of acquired organisations. This can manifest itself in situations where the power structures of the company are highly decentralised and regional managers enjoy a high degree of autonomy and independence.

Some business units will want to "run their own race" rather than "towing the company line". This is especially so where different cultures in organisations have not been fully or properly integrated. There are a number of companies where the personnel of a business unit acquired by a larger company, continue to associate and refer to themselves and the business by its pre-acquisition identity. It is not unusual for this to go on for a number of years after the acquisition.

This "us" and "them" view of the world is typically a tell-tale sign of a failure of the post-acquisition integration process. There are many acquisition transactions where no such formal integration plans or process were ever implemented.

More <u>centralised</u> control structures may be needed in such instances.

This was one of the problems that Lou Gerstner found at IBM when he first assumed the role of CEO in 1993. One of his first acts of reorganisation was to give his country managers less independence and introduce a much more centralised model.

Corporate governance and compliance

There are three factors of central importance to an effective corporate compliance program:

1. It is important that any program have a strong educative element so that employees actually receive practical, useful information about how to identify and avoid common legal problems and compliance issues. Seminars and training are the most obvious tool to use in accomplishing this objective.

2. The program must have a monitoring component, so that there is an effective audit of whether the corporation is complying with its own compliance program.

3. There must be clearly established disciplinary actions, in the event of non-compliance.

Good corporate governance requires a board to create an incentive and accountability system within the enterprise that rewards compliance with the law. In many cases corporate employees either do not appreciate the potential liability risks of certain conduct or are not motivated to reduce those risks.

Shareholders demand good corporate governance because the costs of non-compliance will always far outweigh the costs incurred in developing and implementing a thorough and effective compliance programme.

Good corporate governance is also demanded by the increasingly complex regulatory framework within which most businesses now operate.

The potential costs of failing to comply are threefold:

1. financial – in the form of fines etc;
2. regulatory – in the form of non-financial sanctions and possible imprisonment terms; and
3. adverse public-relations impact upon the firm (with its consequent impact upon the company's share price).

Compliance programs are just frameworks for the actual process of educating corporate employees about the need for compliance and managing the implementation of that process.

Decentralising contract evaluations

This of course refers to a situation where an organisation has its contracts evaluated by (usually non-legal) persons who are not based at the operating company's head office – who also do not have a direct reporting line to head office executive management.

A typical situation might be a company with its head office in London and other offices scattered across major centres within Britain – contract reviews for contracts in the Midlands would be performed in Birmingham, in Liverpool for the North, etc.

The inherent danger of decentralising the evaluation of contracts is the establishment of parameters. Sufficient parameters are difficult to define and require constant monitoring to ensure they are being complied with. Measuring contractual risk by dollar value alone is not always a true indicator.

Often, the extent of the monitoring (by Head Office) required for decentralized contract reviews can lead to a wasteful duplication of efforts, in laboriously re-checking contracts after the event.

It is unrealistic to expect non-legal personnel to assume the mantle of a lawyer by arming them with a simple "how-to" manual and a seminar. It is unfair to expect these people to make a correct "borderline" call or sometimes to even recognise that a case may be more complex than it appears.

In a decentralised model, there is a risk that the role of senior management is reduced to policing and monitoring *after the event*. Often, by the time an act of non-compliance is discovered, the organisation may be committed to a contract and it could be too late to avert the relevant consequences.

Organisations need to move away from a defensive and *reactive* role of catching people out "doing the wrong thing". A more *proactive* stance is a more ideal way of leading an organisation toward compliance.

Unfortunately, many organisations, whilst unwilling to spend money on prevention, willingly spend large amounts of time and money fixing a problem that has manifested itself, because of the immediacy and necessity of achieving a solution. This is because such (after the event) spending will produce a tangible result.

Front-end preventative measures do not have the direct *appearance* of generating any demonstrable savings on the bottom line at the end of each month. However, such preventative measures work best when they are seamless and inconspicuous.

Rectifying problems at the "back-end" (after the worst has happened) is always more costly and disruptive to an organisation. The cost goes beyond the dollar value of the "fix" alone. There is the loss of productivity, the potential loss of reputation etc.

Another of the dangers faced by organisations is the operation of a number of business relationships (often, long standing ones) without any, or any adequate, form of contract document. In a decentralized environment, this is much more difficult to monitor and correct.

Organisations that can benefit from decentralising are those of a certain size that might have a lawyer within that decentralised business unit, who can understand head office materiality criteria (what is really important to the organisation) and parameters, to effectively manage the review of contracts accordingly.

Chapter 7

CONTRACT MANAGEMENT SOLUTIONS

▓▓▓

Of course, choosing whether to centralise or to decentralise the function of contract evaluation will depend upon the size of the organisation, the nature of the business it conducts and even, to some extent, the inherent culture of an organisation. There is no "one size fits all" way to achieve a proper result. It requires expertise, objectivity and experience to do so.

Some organisations will benefit from one approach over the other. Some may even find a workable compromise by blending the two approaches into a well-defined system and process.

Checklist: tailoring a contract management solution to an organisation

The design of a contract management solution will firstly require a careful and thorough analysis to establish answers to the following questions:

• What is the company's philosophy?

• What are the attitudes of the company and senior management toward compliance matters?

• Does the company operate offensively or defensively? Is it proactive or reactive?

• Does the legal department advise on how to avoid trouble or does it wait until the ship hits the rocks before trying to save it?

• What is the cultural "fit" to the organisation of any solution, in order to ensure its effectiveness?

• How does management make decisions, gather information, interact with employees and deal with significant issues?

Indeed, some organisations dealing with a large volume of contracts, may make it necessary to formulate a policy dealing with "material" contracts only. The skill and expertise required in such an instance is the arrival at a proper definition of the categories that will actually constitute a "material" contract, in order to warrant a full evaluation.

Other organisations may prefer all major deals to be referred to a contracts committee for approval. The committee typically consists of a broad cross-section of senior individuals within the organisation. For example, it would usually include, at a minimum, the CEO and CFO together with a corporate counsel and a commercial director.

Such a committee could also designate and appoint a particular person or persons from within the organisation to negotiate the contract terms of a major deal with the other party. It may not necessarily be the person who "put the deal together" or brought the business into the organisation. Doing so, thereby introduces another layer of "checks and balances".

The initial catalyst to examining the issue in many organisations is, firstly, the realisation that it has a problem with the management of contracts. This could be triggered by circumstances such as:

- litigation into which the organisation was dragged;
- the first-time appointment of an in-house lawyer to that organisation; or
- an external consultant's report.

It is comparatively rare for an organisation to actually come to such a realisation without a fresh set of eyes viewing and assessing the systems and procedures in place.

Once the need is established, a solution specifically tailored to the organisation's specific requirements, should be devised. Generally, the process of a typical contract management project tends to unfold in three distinct phases.

░

Steps in a contract management project

Phase one

Phase one of the project is usually a survey phase. This phase is used to formulate the nature and extent of the problem confronting an organisation. Usually, the information gathered in this phase tends to "open a few eyes" at the Board levels of the organisation.

From a practical perspective, this phase is undertaken by surveying a number of selected managers at various levels to obtain a representative cross-section of the organisation's day-to-day operations.

The careful drafting of the survey document is of critical importance to the end result. The survey is critical to encourage management "buy in" of the process and may promote its acceptance as a consultative implementation. Failure to do so may create a real risk that acceptance of the project might not ultimately be achieved.

Site visits are normally undertaken after the completion of the survey, to discuss the results with the various managers. This discussion part of the phase enables the upper executive management and the Board to understand the story behind the answers given in the survey.

Phase two

Phase two consists of a thorough analysis of all survey and interview responses, through which a scope of works is produced. This phase requires skill and judgment, which helps to identify the most appropriate direction for the organisation to take. The scope of works maps out the contract management solution and is a detailed blueprint to be followed for the implementation in the next phase.

Phase three

Phase three is the execution phase where the project finally comes together. Organisations now start to see a tangible result. The deliverables of this stage are usually:

1. the forms of the contracts themselves that are drafted and readied. Wherever possible, they should be written in "plain English";

2. the explanatory guides that are produced regarding the new forms and their use;

3. the training programmes that are conducted on the new forms of contract, to demonstrate their most effective use and familiarise the end-users;

4. the rollout of 1) and 2) above to the relevant people *on-line* through a corporate intranet.

The Outcome

A successful project should culminate in:

- the production and implementation of standard forms of contract for use throughout each legal jurisdiction of the organisation. These would then be centrally maintained and updated;

- all business units throughout each legal jurisdiction having access to the same up to date forms;

- a defined and uniform set of parameters within which contracts can be negotiated;

- site visits and instruction on the use of the standard forms and explanation of how the parameters devised will assist;

- a centralised contract and document management system and policy; and

- a central point of access and co-ordination for all contract problems and queries. Usually, the in-house lawyer becomes this resource.

▌▌▌

Standard forms of contract

To optimise their impact and usability, standard forms of contract must:

- cater to the needs of each business;

- be flexible enough to accommodate various options;

- maximise the organisation's legal position;

- reflect variations in local laws (if the organisation encompasses more than a single legal jurisdiction);

- be in plain language and easy to use;

- be recognisable as a document emanating from the organisation.

The following areas of an organisation should consider it mandatory to have a suite of standard forms of contract:

- human resources;

- operations; and

- purchasing and procurement.

Now we have standard forms of contract: the next steps

Do not be fooled into thinking that standard forms are a universal panacea to good contract management. Standard forms used inappropriately, can be severely detrimental to an organisation. Conversely, having the world's best (and most expensive to produce) forms available that sit on a shelf and are never used, are just as bad a result for an organisation.

To achieve success in implementing a contract management solution, it is not enough for the documents themselves to be carefully drafted. Their introduction to the relevant staff-members must be done in a structured manner to ensure the staff acquire a sound working knowledge and understanding of the documents.

A structured training programme for the staff of an organisation should be able to produce an understanding of:

- the organisation's contract management policy;
- the use and purpose of each contract;
- the requirement for each variable;
- the provision of alternative clauses for use in negotiations;

- the potential legal issues in each contract and the potential effect of indiscriminate departures from the contract or the contract management policy; and

- clear boundaries for critical items that the organisation will always insist upon as non-negotiable items.

In this manner, they will be more comfortable with the use of the documents and will be able to handle most customer queries "on the spot" and professionally.

The success of the system is where it is regarded as a useful tool by the people who use it, rather than being seen as an impediment to doing business.

The ultimate aim, ideally, is to have the relevant contracts available to a business on-line through a corporate intranet. In this way, the latest version of a contract document would always be available to the end-user. This version could be updated centrally (whenever required) and then be instantly made available to all users. Modification of the documents can be controlled and monitored. It is possible to give different levels of management clearance to amend certain parts of the document and not other parts.

The electronic suite of documents delivered by corporate intranet (or even on CD-ROM for those organisations without a corporate intranet), avoids the traditional problems of superceded versions of contracts "gathering dust" or being used incorrectly instead of the latest forms.

It also generates considerable savings on printing and distribution costs.

▌▌▌

Document execution form

Such a form is typically a snapshot summary of the main highlights of the contract, of relevance and importance to the contract signatory:

- Brief summary of the nature of the contract
- Key deal terms
- Length of time the company is committed to the contract
- Financial impact summary
- Key risk areas
- Details of who has reviewed the document
- Details of those who have formally approved the company entering into the document
- Compliance with company policy
- Areas which deviate from company policy and an explanation of why the company is proceeding and who authorised same to proceed.

In organisations, documents are generally executed by a company director or company secretary in a central corporate function. Often the document arrives with a simple memo (or sometimes, even a post-it note saying "please sign and return" – a scary prospect in a multinational organisation!).

The person signing can often have no idea of what the document is about and who has approved it, without reading it. Reading every word of the document does not always give the reader an understanding of the internal organisational approval processes the document has been through (or *should* have gone through).

A document execution form is used, as a uniform way of bringing up questions/issues which should always be asked by any person with the responsibility to execute documents on behalf of an organisation:

- Is there capital expenditure involved?

- How long (for what term) does it commit the company?

- Is the expenditure within the manager's level of authority to approve?

- Has there been legal, accounting or tax advice obtained on particular aspects of the document?

- Who has read the contract?

- Who understands it and takes responsibility for the organisation performing to it?

- Are there consequential loss provisions?

- What are the liability provisions?

- What protections/safeguards are engineered into the document?

- What are the termination/exit provisions

These are all vitally important questions to understand before a company executes any contract.

If an organisation does nothing else but implement and enforce the use of such a document execution form, it is already doing something valuable and worthwhile in minimising its legal risk exposure. Just a simple form such as this one becomes a powerful compliance tool creating accountability and responsibility for transactions. It encourages analysis; by the simple discipline of preparing a proper summary by the person who put the deal together. It encourages further scrutiny, by the person ultimately signing the contract, in verifying these steps.

This form is also a good corporate governance discipline and useful audit tool. The form can be adapted to suit specific requirements. A prime example would be the addition of a section into the form on capital expenditure requirements and authorisations.

Note that some organisations keep it to a single A4 sized page deliberately, to encourage it to be used.

If it is longer, it can sometimes act as a deterrent to usage. People will start to view the document as "more red tape and bureaucracy". I have seen some forms routinely used by some multinationals to be multi-paged affairs. The point is that having one is better than not having one.

Indeed, when I was the company secretary of one multinational corporation, with my territory extending over 14 separate legal jurisdictions, it was my established practice to not even contemplate signing a contract, without a properly completed document execution form. Once managers realised that this was the only way to get things done, they soon adapted to the practice. Indeed, many later confided what a good idea they thought it was and how using the form often brought significant matters to their attention, of which they would have otherwise been unaware.

Beware the persons who complain about the time it takes to properly complete such a form – they usually tend to be the ones who prefer to take short-cuts and are not across the detail of their portfolio.

Chapter 8

CONTRACT MAINTENANCE

▓▓▓▓

Once drafted, standard terms should not be "laid to rest", but should be reviewed regularly. The world of business is constantly changing and evolving and a company's standard form of contract reflects the extent to which a company keeps pace with such change.

Over time, businesses will expand into (or downsize from) particular strategic areas and geographic locations. A company's products will also change over time, as will the way that competitors deal. If competitors start offering more generous terms, a company will have to review its positions to maintain (or at least not lose) any of its competitive advantage.

Contracts must also keep pace with any significant changes in the law (or its interpretation) and allow a company to profit from any experience gained "in the field". This avoids repetition of costly mistakes and the actual prevention of others.

Employees in the organisation should be encouraged to assist and contribute in keeping documents up to date. Their suggestions should be actively sought by an organisation by use of suggestion boxes or as part of a more structured appraisal process.

▓▓▓

A basic compliance system

A contract management solution produces benefits and savings generated by the organisation's increased certainty of compliance and its customers' confidence in the integrity and reputation of the organisation. The benefits are clear and tangible. There are also the additional benefits of potential savings in the reduced number of contract disputes and litigation.

Most organisations will benefit from developing a proper compliance manual covering, at least, the following areas:

- any specific product licencing;
- workplace relations;
- occupational health and safety;

- anti-discrimination and harassment;

- trade practices, competition and anti-trust;

- professional indemnity;

- directors and officers liability; and

- contracts management procedure.

In addition to having appropriate manuals and guidelines, there must be adequate implementation of processes to ensure they become a part of a manager's daily life and do not simply sit on a shelf gathering dust.

Such implementation, as a minimum, should consist of at least:

- ensuring the relevant staff are familiar with its contents by developing and conducting a structured training programme;

- formulating a policy regarding the evaluation of incoming contracts;

- formulating a policy regarding levels of authority to enter into certain types of agreements without the need to refer to head office. For example, depending on the length of the term of a proposed contract, the amount of any capital expenditure required for a particular project, the types of goods or services being provided (particularly if they are non-core to the organisation). See the case study in the final chapter illustrating this point;

- diffusing such policies throughout the organisation ensuring that they are understood to be mandatory;

- the establishment of a centralised database listing every license and piece of intellectual property the organisation holds. This list should be maintained centrally and procedures established for each site or business unit to update relevant changes to the database;

- the establishment of crisis teams and appropriate guidelines and policies.

One multinational spared no expense in developing a corporate code of conduct with input from lawyers all over the world. It was a beautiful and impressive document, which covered a lot of ground.

However, the code was certain to fail because of the lack of a clear implementation plan. Each relevant manager was destined to sign-off on the document on an annual basis during an audit. As such, this virtually guaranteed that the document would be considered no more than once-a-year during a routine "box ticking" exercise.

A better way might have been to unveil it to the relevant staff by the chief executive and ensuring that compliance was tied to each manager's bonus or incentive scheme plan.

▓▓▓

Contract management policy

A well-constructed contract management policy should effectively deal with the following issues:

- levels of contract review and signoff based on the level of risk associated with a contract. Remember, that basing a risk assessment of a contract on dollar value alone is dangerous;

- tender bidding procedures;

- introduction and use of standard forms of contract;

- document execution procedures. The use of a document execution form such as that reproduced in this chapter, in the manner discussed;

- document security;

- document retention;

- document destruction; and

- a manual *and* education programme covering all of the above.

A contract management system with a higher level of information technology integration is obviously more desirable in producing a more functional system.

This might incorporate diary reminders to flag key dates such as renewal dates, price increases and billing cycles. Also, record retention dates could be flagged to aid in this function (eg destroying records over a certain age).

Chapter 9

WHO REVIEWS THE CONTRACTS?

Some companies have their own in-house legal resources (ranging from a sole junior lawyer to a team of seasoned and experienced counsel). Other companies must either divide the function amongst commercial personnel and/or contract work out to external lawyers. Often a blend of these situations occur in the day-to-day running of a large commercial enterprise.

All too often, the resource of the in-house legal counsel is over-worked and under-utilised. Whilst this might, at first, seem paradoxical, what it in fact means, is that most in-house counsel are kept extremely busy on mostly lower-level and low-value tasks.

An in-house lawyer can be a valuable resource to the benefit of the organisation, without requiring them to work 18-hour days, six days per week. A number of CEOs do not extract that value.

Regardless of where your company sits on this issue there is always the opportunity to review and improve the functionality of these roles.

▓▓▓

Role of the in-house lawyer

The corporate lawyer adds value to an organisation as an advisor to management and a provider of legal services. Both functions will be explored below.

Legal advisor to management

A lawyer can be a situation or transaction dependent advisor, advising senior management on individual matters such as mergers, acquisitions, joint ventures, and the impact of a particular piece of legislation on a particular proposed transaction.

The lawyer can use legal foresight to identify trends in the law and how they will impact the company's business over time. The evolution of the law applicable to human resource matters is a classic example of where the lawyer's futurist role is critically important. Wrongful termination, passive smoking, equal opportunity employment, anti-discrimination, sexual harassment and patent trolling are but a few of the legal areas likely to have a dramatic impact on the conduct of business.

In order to make a key contribution to the future economic health and well-being of a business entity, a forward looking lawyer should:

- identify trends;
- evaluate their likelihood of occurrence;
- devise legal solutions to probable changes;
- alert management to the changes for the purpose of devising business strategies in response to them.

A lawyer can participate in the strategic planning process. The lawyer must alert management to legal trends so that the managers may plan and avoid pitfalls. In this capacity, the strategic planning process becomes legally driven. The impact of the law on the business process is very real. No strategic plan can be developed which does not include the legal ramifications of the proposed conduct. To be effective, the earlier and the more involved that the lawyer becomes in this process, the more likely it is that she will be able to provide meaningful advice and help avoid problems.

As management develops its strategic business plans, the corporate lawyer must participate in the planning process in order to produce programmes which are legally feasible or do not have an exceptionally high level of legal risk associated with them.

Provider of functional legal services

The corporate lawyer is also called upon to provide cost effective and functional day-to-day services. The nature of these services in most companies generally includes:

- handling routine day-to-day legal matters (eg, leases, contracts, confidentiality agreements, contractual notices, correspondence);

- managing litigation; and

- conducting and controlling special projects such as contract negotiations, acquisitions and disposals;

- selecting and retaining external lawyers.

Growing volumes of work

Most in-house legal roles tend to be purely functional and therefore limited by the sheer volume of the day-to-day workload. This effectively eliminates a significant proportion of the value that a competent general counsel can add to the business and its processes.

Some subsidiaries see the in-house lawyer's function simply as a free legal resource to tap into and produce budget savings for them.

As the burden of the day-to-day functional work becomes overwhelming, the in-house lawyer does not get to visit, spend time with and develop proper relationships and understandings with each part of the business. The reason for this is that the lawyer spends their entire time being *reactive* to subsidiaries' request for assistance. As a result, they tend to have very little involvement in the affairs of any of the businesses beyond the company's head office.

Such a role risks becoming oriented from the bottom-up, rather than being a top-down role.

What this means, is that the bulk of the lawyer's time is dedicated to minutiae of subsidiaries wishing to obtain free legal advice, instead of a proactive head-office high value role, with direct involvement in major transactions affecting the group.

As with any other part of the business, the CEO must always take an appropriate opportunity to reconsider and redesign the in-house legal role to improve upon the value that it is capable of generating and achieving for the corporate group.

▥

Lawyers as advisers

The cardinal rule to remember when dealing with lawyers is that *they do not make decisions; they advise.* Do not lose sight of this fundamental and critical fact. Commercial and contract decisions are ultimately made by managers, not their lawyers.

On occasions, deals can be lost because commercial people abdicate responsibility to their lawyers or, worse still, the lawyers decide that they know what is right for the company and therefore decide on commercial matters for the client.

Any deal involves risk. If a lawyer is given too wide a brief, there is a risk of derailing a deal. The lawyer's role is to protect the client and that is where an out-of-control lawyer can start inserting clauses or warranties into an agreement that are designed to protect, but might otherwise ignore the context or spirit of the deal.

If they are trusted and have a track record of being commercially astute with you, you can allow them a degree of latitude and autonomy on their assessment of legal matters. Often the lawyer can be used in difficult contract negotiations to play the "bad cop" role. Using this approach, the lawyer raises strenuous objections to key negotiation points and the commercial person overrules them, as the "good cop".

Checklist:
when to allow lawyers to lead negotiations

Lawyers should only be allowed to lead contract negotiations where they are fully familiar with:

- all relevant aspects of the deal;

- the nature of the industry (what is common usage and what is not);

- commercial sensitivities involved;

- strategic imperatives on achieving the deal; and

- the cost of not doing the deal, as well as the cost of doing the deal and it going badly.

Provided always, that they defer to management to make the ultimate decision.

Streamlining the use of internal legal departments

The manner in which the company's business units interact and develop a relationship with the in-house lawyer is a large determinant of the success, or otherwise, of the in-house legal role.

As such, some legal departments (even if the department consists of a single lawyer) look to develop ways of better servicing the company's business units. One particularly effective method is the development of a simple user's guide to legal services. The idea is to encourage the use of the service, but to ensure that requests for assistance follow a proper pre-determined channel. This ensures that the resource is not abused by the few who think of it as a "free ride" and that the requests for assistance are focused ones. A sample users' guide has been included for your perusal in *Appendix A*.

▌▌▌

DIY legal services

If your company is a start-up or is too small to require the services of a full-time lawyer, decisions will still need to be made as to how contract reviews are performed and by whom.

Questions you need to ask include:

- Who takes responsibility for legal decisions?

- Does a different department take responsibility for commercial decisions?

- How, if at all, are external lawyers to be used?

- Is there to be a selection or panel of external lawyers to be used?

- In what circumstances will matters be referred for external legal advice?

- Who within the company is to be the conduit for and to manage such referrals?

- Should head office take responsibility for the review of contracts, or should the function more properly reside within each subsidiary?

Persons responsible for the interface with the customer (typically sales or operations staff) sometimes perform contract reviews and make decisions on what clauses to accept or reject. The rationale behind this decision is that operations staff will end up actually providing the goods and/or services that are the subject of the contract, therefore, they are best placed to know whether they will be able to work to the contract. Certainly, the input of both sales and operations people is always useful and valuable in relation to assessing the viability of commercial aspects of a deal. Their value, however, will not usually extend to providing a proper assessment of the *legal* aspects and risks of a particular transaction.

If such staff are to deal with contracts, adequate and workable parameters need to be set for them. These are difficult to define and require constant monitoring to ensure compliance. For example, if your organisation assesses which contract may be handled by the subsidiary based on its dollar value as the only parameter, this can be a dangerous thing. An indemnity in a small dollar value contract could have a massive impact, as you'll see in the example below.

Case study
How the failure of a hundred dollar part derails a nation's space programme

Titan Uranus was the supplier of a small specialised rubber sealing component that cost only a few dollars to produce.

The component was to be used in a country's space programme in a part of the spacecraft's rocket engine assembly. A failure in the component could lead to a failure in the entire spacecraft with catastrophic consequences.

The supply contract called for the supply of a hundred of these components at a cost of several thousand dollars each. The dollar value of the contract is therefore on the very low end of Titan Uranus' scale of revenue producing activities.

Imagine, as part of the space programme's supply contract, that Titan Uranus is required to indemnify (take legal responsibility) against the effects of failure of the component.

The contract, which only generates a few hundreds of thousand dollars in revenue, now carries potentially billions of dollars in risk. It raises the stakes considerably doesn't it? Titan's directors would certainly be taking the action suggested by the company's name, before entering into such a contract.

> Assessing that contract to be a low-risk one, based on its dollar value alone, becomes a foolish exercise, if not a grossly negligent or reckless one.

Sales and operations people are driven by priorities and motivations other than legal concerns.

In the case of sales staff, the zeal to close a deal may, in some instances, compromise the judgment of that salesperson into accepting unduly onerous terms. Often, the rewards of salespersons are based on the number of deals and/or the volume of business brought into the organisation. The organisation's compliance with the terms of contract then becomes someone else's problem. Therefore, allowing commission-based salespeople to be the sole evaluators of incoming contracts, could be said by some, to be akin to allowing the proverbial wolf to guard the chickens.

Whereas, operations personnel may (with the best of intentions) be tempted to think that they can overcome a badly-worded contract document, by good management and impeccable customer service. Unfortunately, the reality is that relationships cannot always overcome bad contract terms.

Case study: how differing interests affect decision-making

Operations

Business manager, **Terry Fide**, lives and dies by his monthly numbers. He has little interest in making longer-term investment decisions. It's not his fault he thinks this way as most line managers like Terry are judged and held accountable to their monthly numbers.

Terry's department has a high number of worker injuries and escalating insurance premiums.

Management's knee-jerk reaction is to get tough on such malingering workers. The organisation is then seen as less sympathetic to the injured worker and general morale plummets, as a result.

It may have been more appropriate to renew the focus on occupational health and safety prevention and training. In the end this doesn't produce a bottom-line return in the following month, so Terry doesn't consider it.

Terry is tempted to make significant concessions when negotiating an indemnity clause, since he perceives that it doesn't have any immediate bottom-line effect. In the end the company is sued for negligence for taking on responsibility for something that would not have otherwise been its fault.

A better scenario would have been to draw a budget with provisions for these kinds of longer-term investment strategies. This is especially so where long-term solutions are being implemented to address causes, rather than reactive expenditures to plug obvious holes. Managers' incentive programmes should be designed with the types of decisions that produce long-term benefits to an organisation.

Business development (sales)

In the organisation **'Hugh G. Rection Constructions PLC'** ("HGR"), the emphasis of HGR's Sales Director, **Annie Rupshen**, is on winning new business and boosting top-line revenues, rather than on the quality and profit-ability of those contracts.

From ten new contracts won by sales staff of HGR, only two turn out to be profitable. In reality, Anne tends to mask the unprofitable ones by setting them off against the sky high profits earned in the two profitable ones.

The difficulty here lies in correctly identifying and attributing the responsibility for any such unprofitability (eg, whether it was due to a change in circumstances, incorrect estimating, or whether the operations side of the contract is being badly managed, etc).

Ideally, incentive structures could be geared towards a shift to attracting and retaining only profitable business and to jettison the unprofitable ones.

Incentives could be linked to both individual and global profitability of all contracts generated by the business development/sales team.

The only way to maintain control over the outcome of the contract review process is for management to have a policy in place at the *front end* of the process and to enforce it. A necessary part of this is ensuring that the appropriate persons have a working knowledge of the policy and of the benefits it produces for them.

It is unrealistic to expect non-legal personnel to assume the mantle of a lawyer by arming them with a simple 'how-to' manual and a seminar. It is unfair to expect these people to make a correct 'borderline' call or sometimes to even recognise that a contract clause may be more complex than it first appears.

In this model, there is a risk that the role of senior management is reduced to policing and monitoring *after the event.* Often, by the time an act of non-compliance is discovered, the organisation may be committed to it and it could be too late to avert the relevant consequences. Laboriously re-checking contracts after the event is often also a wasteful duplication of efforts, inherent in this DIY system.

Unfortunately, many organisations, whilst unwilling to spend money on prevention, willingly spend large amounts of time and money fixing a problem that has manifested itself, because of the immediacy and necessity of achieving a solution.

But rectifying problems at the 'back-end', or, after the worst has happened is always more costly and disruptive to an organisation. The cost extends beyond the dollar value of the 'fix' alone to include loss of productivity, the potential loss of reputation, etc.

Another of the dangers faced by organisations is the operation of a number of business relationships (often, long standing ones) without any, or any adequate, form of contract document. This is more often the danger where business units are left to their own devices.

Combining the approaches

One solution to this problem could be to categorise issues that could be dealt with by managers, and those that must be dealt with by legal departments. Issues can either be legal or commercial. This is an important distinction.

For example, if a manager wishes to make a price concession in a contract negotiation (assuming the manager can still 'make the numbers'), the issue should have nothing to do with the lawyers and should remain the responsibility of the manager or their superior.

By the same token, managers should not seek to absolve themselves from all decision-making responsibility or consequences by having lawyers sign off on everything; even on issues that are not strictly legal ones.

The difference between commercial decisions and legal issues

There are differing categories of issues that require evaluation. Issues can either be legal or commercial. This is an important distinction.

It is that distinction that divides issues that need to be dealt with by lawyers and those that are commercial terms that can require decisions to be made by managers. For example, if a manager wishes to make a price concession in a contract negotiation - assuming the manager can still "make his numbers", the issue should have nothing to do with the lawyers and should remain the responsibility of the manager or their superior.

By the same token, managers should not seek to absolve themselves from all decision-making responsibility or consequences by having lawyers sign off on everything; even on issues that are not strictly legal ones.

Case Study: Sue Ridge Publishing PLC

Commercial decision or legal issue?

Let us consider some common parameters which line managers can acceptably deal with.

For example, consider the situation of a book publishing company, Sue Ridge Publishing PLC. Many critics have described many of their books as "excrement". However, they have managed to snare the author of the leading guide to Sports Fishing in Britain, **Barry Mundy**. This title is regarded as a great "catch" in the publishing industry and would be the jewel in their crown, helping them revive their sullied reputation in the industry.

The author **Barry Mundy**, is negotiating his contract for the publisher to release the latest revised edition of Barry's respected and revered tome.

Depending on the publisher, an acquisitions editor only has limited (if any) authority to vary certain commercial terms of a publishing contract.

Let us look at five separate situations that now confront the acquisitions editor, **Rod**

Denreel, in his efforts to secure the rights for **Sue Ridge Publishing PLC** to publish this most sought-after book. Barry thinks he has the upper hand in the negotiations now that he has this publisher on the hook. However, he is keen to avoid anything "fishy" in his publishing contract and is wary of any attempt by his publisher to bait-and-switch him:

1) **Barry** requires the assignment of all copyright in the work to himself, as the author;

2) **Barry** has requested that the royalty payable on book sales be increased from 10% to 15%;

3) **Barry** wishes to have 1,000 extra free copies of the book, as competition giveaways on his TV show;

4) **Barry** has requested an additional advertising campaign contribution from the publisher of £50,000.

5) **Barry** declines to grant the publisher an indemnity in respect of the originality of the work;

Of the five situations listed, which are those that are effectively commercial decisions for **Rod**, which are likely to only have a budgetary (£) impact alone and not affect the publisher's legal position?

The answer is that situations 2, 3 and 4 would appear to be commercial decisions that could be safely made by **Rod** (assuming he has the requisite internal authority).

Issues 2, 3, and 4 do not require legal input. For example, giving **Barry Mundy** 1,000 extra free books does not legally prejudice the publisher. It is simply a question of pounds and pence.

Whereas, the question of *copyright* in situation number 1 is an intellectual property issue.

The *indemnity* question in issue 5 is definitely a legal issue.

These and other similar contract variations sought by **Barry** should, ideally, be submitted to the legal department and the CEO of the publisher to seek further advice on the legal and commercial ramifications.

Chapter 10

CONCLUSION

By now, you will have gained an appreciation of some of the micro hot-spots of specific contract clauses and some tricks and traps on which to be alert.

You have witnessed the typical steps through which a business must proceed in order to make a proper assessment of whether to enter into a contract and if so, on what terms.

We have journeyed through the compliance systems of organisations and considered the context of the contract management system within the greater compliance system unit.

Unfortunately, a number of organisations (both large and small) do not pay sufficient attention to contract evaluation processes, often to their detriment. You have now seen examples of the consequences of such lapses and have gained some insight into avoiding their repetition – especially if you begin to see the early warning signs in your organisation.

By now, you should be in a position to be able to consider the merits and disadvantages – as they relate to your particular organisation – of whether to centralise or decentralise the contract evaluation process. You will now understand the impact each method has (depending upon the organisation's structure and culture), on the effectiveness, or otherwise, of the contract evaluation process.

You should know some of the things required in a contract to provide basic safeguards. You should also be better able to ascertain when another party is being overzealous or overstepping the bounds of reason-ableness in their drafting of such a document.

The intricate relationship between the contract evaluation process and the risk being assumed by the business, should also, by now, be clear.

Ideally, you have gained an appreciation of the relevant steps required to critically evaluate and scrutinise contracts (with your organisation's particular needs, requirement and capabilities in mind) prior to accepting them.

By this time, any reader should also be "sold" on the merits of having *systems and processes* in place for contract evaluation. Such systems and processes – particularly in larger organisations – can help eliminate the personality influences that can sometimes lead to unnecessary departures from company policies and quality assurance procedures. If allowed to occur, such unauthorised departures tend to detract from the professional image of the organisation.

Such systems and processes also help to "smooth-over" the wide variance in competency levels inherent in any large organisation, that might otherwise tend to undermine organisational consistency.

You should consider the following case study, which illustrates a fundamental point made earlier; how contract management systems can be an aid to keeping an organisation "on course" (even in terms of its core-business activities), in assessing the kinds of contracts it takes on.

CASE STUDY: Cleaning up or cleaned out – what do cleaners know about plastic explosives?

Or, what is my core competency?

A case in point: how does a large organisation control the types of contracts that its sales force wins?

Squeaky Kleen, a large commercial cleaning company, was negotiating to provide its core competency cleaning services to a major regional airport.

During the discussions and negotiations with the airport authority, **Willy Maykit**, an entrepreneurial manager employed by **Squeaky Kleen,** saw the opportunity of also providing other services at the airport (such as x-ray baggage screening).

Willy's reasoning was that x-ray baggage screening was an automated task utilising low-skilled labour, in much the same way as their commercial cleaning operations. The only training required (this occurred prior to September 11, 2001) was a rudimentary familiarisation course on the x-ray screening machine.

Willy figured **Squeaky Kleen** could derive huge economies of scale in providing both of these services required by the airport. In fact, **Willy** even planned to use **Squeaky Kleen's** existing cleaning staff to operate the x-ray screening machines! In Willy's mind, this would generate a cost-savings windfall to the company.

The contract with the airport authority provided that **Squeaky Kleen** would be liable for all losses (including consequential losses) sustained by anyone as a result of any dangerous article or object introduced into an aircraft.

Crucially, the contract contained no qualification by excluding dangerous objects introduced airside (say, by an airport staff member or one of hundreds of other contractors having airside access). Those airside access points were well behind the x-ray screening point. Furthermore, in the event of a disaster, how could **Squeaky Kleen** prove that an explosive device was *not* missed in the screening process? The onus would effectively be upon **Squeaky Kleen** to demonstrate that the object was introduced onto the aircraft by another means. This would be a virtually impossible task in a large airport, where literally thousands of persons could have had such airside access, such as baggage handlers, airline caterers, maintenance staff etc.

Aside from the monumental human tragedy, imagine the quantum of the loss, in dollar terms. What does a large commercial airliner cost to replace? Hundreds of millions of dollars. What about the hundreds (or even thousands) of lives that could be lost in an airline tragedy?

The company failed to consider issues such as aircraft hijackings and other forms of terrorism. Or even dealing with such things as concealed explosives and weaponry, which demand highly specialised forms of military or para-military expertise and intelligence-gathering systems. Such expertise is not readily available; and certainly not to your average cleaning contractor.

Willy's boss, **Betty Wont**, a board-level signatory, brought the contract to the attention of **Cliff Hanga** (**Squeaky Kleen's** in-house lawyer) for a "routine once-over", before signature. **Betty's** only element of doubt in the deal was a complex price-escalation clause.

Fortunately, a last minute review of the contract by **Cliff** gave rise to a comprehensive and detailed advice to **Betty** and the entire board on the potential risks of this contract.

The board of **Squeaky Kleen** accepted **Cliff's** advice and immediately authorised **Betty** to intervene and withdraw the company's tender bid, which had already been submitted to the airport authority. Such withdrawal caused the company considerable embarrassment. However, that was a small price to pay compared to the potential consequences to the company, had it been held responsible for an airline disaster occurring.

This is perhaps one of the more significant examples of a company failing to understand and accurately measure risk, due to its lack of knowledge of the different industry (and its inherent risks) in which it was proposing to dabble.

Squeaky Kleen had a reputation for encouraging a "laissez faire" entrepreneurial approach in its managers. It was also notorious for not having any degree of corporate governance to speak of or if possessing any developed internal regulatory systems. This combination of factors in any organisation is a sure-fire recipe for disaster.

The "checks-and-balances" must always be there.

This is a clear demonstration of the consequences of not having effective contract management policies and evaluation procedures in place. Proper contract evaluation procedures would have intercepted this issue (and immediately brought it to board-level attention) well before the waste of thousands of man-hours in preparing the final tender bid and submitting it to the airport authority.

Just remember, when it comes to contracts:

- <u>everything</u> matters;

- <u>everything</u> counts;

- <u>everything</u> is done (or not done) for a reason;

- <u>every single word </u>can affect the meaning or interpretation of a contract.

- a signature is <u>never</u> a formality. It can often be the very act that locks you in, that binds you to a promise.

Always pause and think before that last step. Check, re-check and triple check.

It may take you time, but so will sitting around a courtroom and sitting in the witness box – being grilled for hours (or perhaps days) under cross examination by an opposing counsel.

Golden Nugget

All it takes...

I was once involved in a case where a company was sued for almost $100million. The case lasted over 3 years and eventually cost the company millions of dollars in legal costs - even though it won.

Those costs do not factor in an allowance for the lost management time and effort sitting around in lawyers' offices and courtrooms spent trying to recall and relive every discussion and meeting held some 3 years prior. That lost time diverted managers from the present and future issues affecting their business.

This could have been averted by the inclusion of the word "and", which was missing from a vital sub-clause buried within a 200+ page contract.

So, benefit from the (unfortunate) experiences of others, and realise that it ALL matters.

Parting thought to cap off the series...

The 10 Habits of Highly Successful Contract Managers:

1. The <u>wisdom</u> of Solomon

2. The <u>foresight</u> of Nostradamus

3. The <u>ruthlessness</u> of Attila

4. The <u>patience</u> of a saint

5. The <u>care</u> of a parent for their newborn

6. The <u>willingness</u> of a school-teacher to educate

7. The <u>diplomacy</u> of a hostage negotiator

8. The <u>mental toughness</u> of an astronaut

9. The <u>persistence</u> of Christopher Columbus

10. A <u>pessimistic view of the world</u> – anticipating disaster around every corner...

USERS' GUIDE TO LEGAL SUPPORT

▉▉▉

Legal charter

The legal function within The XYZ Company (XYZ Legal) is committed to providing advice and guidance of the highest quality to subsidiary companies and to the XYZ Executive Team. In particular, XYZ Legal will focus on dealing with major exposures from a Group perspective and on providing guidance on significant legal matters.

XYZ Legal will also, on behalf of [PARENT COMPANY], monitor and advise on group issues of compliance and corporate governance.

In performing these functions XYZ Legal is responsible to the XYZ Group General Counsel and the local XYZ Executive.

When XYZ Legal can assist

The intervention of XYZ Legal will be appropriate in cases in which:

- The issue is a significant one from a group perspective; and

- It is cost effective to do so; and

- XYZ Legal can add real value to the process.

If requested, assistance will also be available in relation to the selection and supervision (in appropriate matters) of external lawyers. In addition, if you encounter problems in any relationship with your external lawyers, XYZ Legal can be called upon to assist in providing a satisfactory resolution.

Autonomy of subsidiaries

At all times the ultimate responsibility for ensuring the good conduct of your business unit with respect to corporate governance and legal issues remains with you. XYZ Legal will assist you to operate your business within XYZ Company's policy framework.

How to refer a matter to XYZ Legal

Referrals to XYZ Legal from business units should be from either of the following levels within a business unit:

- CEO;
- CFO;
- Operations Manager.

To facilitate a prompt assessment of the issue, it would be of great assistance if you could provide the following in writing, when referring a matter to XYZ Legal:

1) a brief background to establish the facts behind the issue and placing it in context;

2) a concise statement of the problem and question on which you require assistance;

3) a brief statement of the outcome you hope to achieve;

4) copies of any relevant documents and correspondence.

For items 1), 2) and 3) above, this should preferably be in the form of an email. This method will ensure that if **[LAWYER]** is out of the office or travelling, he will have remote access to your message. **For urgent enquiries or matters, messages should always be copied to [LAWYER'S EXECUTIVE ASSISTANT].**

If any additional documents or information needs to be faxed or couriered, this should be done, in addition to the initial email, **by co-ordinating with [LAWYER'S EXECUTIVE ASSISTANT].**

If there is uncertainty as to whether the issue meets the referral criteria set out above, the escalation internally within the business unit to the level of CEO/CFO/Operations Manager will act as an appropriate filter.

From there, a determination can be made as to whether it is appropriate for XYZ Legal's involvement.

To "bounce" something off XYZ Legal

In any event, business units may always, through the CEO/CFO/Operations Manager levels seek off the cuff advice or guidance on specific issues or to seek recommendations of external law firms, for specific problems.

The outcome of a matter referred to XYZ Legal

Upon escalation of a matter to XYZ Legal, you can expect one of the following outcomes:

1) agreement by XYZ Legal to assume the conduct of an issue of significance, either with or without the assistance of external legal support;

2) a recommendation that the matter be referred to external lawyers by the business unit but under the ongoing supervision of **XYZ Legal**;

3) a recommendation that the matter be handled internally by the business unit, with or without the assistance of external lawyers.

XYZ Legal will endeavour to provide a prompt response to each referral, however, on occasion, prior to receiving a definitive response, you may be asked to provide additional clarification on particular points or desired outcomes.

Questions?

If unsure about any aspect of a problem, it is always best to pick up the telephone and discuss the problem or the issue.

Our contact details are:

INDEX

MANAGERS GUIDE SERIES
COMMERCIAL CONTRACTS FOR MANAGERS

Particular contract clauses (boilerplate clauses) are important in commercial contracts. Some executives will only scrutinise the commercial or "deal" terms of the contract. The rest is usually left for the lawyers. However, the boilerplate clause will usually govern or regulate the other clauses. They play a vital part in the contract.

ISBN: 978-0-85297-758-3   192 pages

You've been involved in weeks, or sometimes even months, of hardfought negotiations. However, the deal is not done until until the final form of contract is agreed upon and executed. You have to have a basic understanding of commercial contracts every step of the way.

ISBN: 978-0-85297-720-0   278 pages

This book explains the essential elements necessary for a complete confidentiality agreement. You will learn how unscrupulous players use confidentiality agreements to gain an unfair advantage, and how to avoid getting "caught".

ISBN: 978-0-85297-757-6   188 pages

This book explains the differences between fair indemnity clauses and those that are unduly onerous and will give readers an understanding of the nature of indemnities and their potentially devastating effects.

ISBN: 978-0-85297-760-6   96 pages

Samples of tender conditions and documents are included to illustrate to the manager capital expenditure, protection of intellectual property and variations to the scopes of works and pricing. The book also explains legal issues, such as liquidated damages, force majeure, indemnities, and so on.

ISBN: 978-0-85297-761-3   144 pages